THE JONES & LAUGHLIN CASE

◄§ BORZOI SERIES §►
IN
UNITED STATES
CONSTITUTIONAL HISTORY

CONSULTING EDITOR:
PAUL MURPHY

UNIVERSITY OF MINNESOTA

The
Jones & Laughlin
Case

RICHARD C. CORTNER

UNIVERSITY OF ARIZONA

ALFRED · A · KNOPF   NEW YORK

Library of Congress Catalog Card Number: 72–120145
Standard Book Number: 394–30294–x

Manufactured in the United States

FIRST EDITION
987654321

Series design by J. M. Wall

FOR

Al Hughes
A Teacher

"The law is like . . . a single-bed blanket on a double bed and three folks in the bed and a cold night. There ain't ever enough blanket to cover the case, no matter how much pulling and hauling, and somebody is always going to nigh catch pneumonia. Hell, the law is like the pants you bought last year for a growing boy, but it is always this year and the seams are popped and the shankbones to the breeze. The law is always too short and too tight for growing humankind. The best you can do is do something and then make up some law to fit and by the time that law gets on the books you would have done something different."

Willie Stark in *All the King's Men*

❦ Preface ❧

The history of the United States has been punctuated at intervals with conflicts of varying degrees of severity between the Supreme Court and the elected branches of the government. The Republic was still in its infancy when such a conflict broke out between the Marshall Court and the political forces led by Thomas Jefferson. This confrontation was to be followed by similar conflicts between Jackson and Marshall, and Lincoln and Taney. The history of National Labor Relations Board v. Jones & Laughlin Steel Corporation, 301 U.S. 1 (1937), is to a very great extent a history of another such conflict—this time between Franklin D. Roosevelt and the Hughes Court of the 1930s.

The *Jones & Laughlin* case was the turning point in the battle that broke out in the spring of 1937 over Roosevelt's attempt to "pack" the Court by adding more Justices who were favorable to the New Deal. He was trying to lift the Court imposed constitutional barriers which had resulted in the invalidation of major New Deal legislation from 1933 to 1937. The *Jones & Laughlin* case was even more significant, however, in modern American constitutional development. For in that and following cases, the Court abandoned its previous role as censor of policies developed by the elected branches of the government in regard to the regulation of the national economy. The *Jones & Laughlin* case also marks the beginning of the Court's focus upon constitutional issues relating to political and civil liberties, the constitutional right to equality, and the problems of criminal procedure that have characterized the most important cases decided by the post-1937 Court.

This history of the *Jones & Laughlin* case is first a history of labor relations in the United States during the 1930s and second a history of the constitutional politics of the New

Deal period. But the *Jones & Laughlin* case is preeminently the history of one of those periodic constitutional cases of momentous significance that mark major turning points in American constitutional development.

An earlier and more general exploration of this subject area was published by the University of Tennessee Press in 1964.* I express my appreciation to the University of Tennessee Press for its permission to utilize materials from that earlier work. A substantial part of my work on the *Jones & Laughlin* case was originally done in connection with the writing of my doctoral dissertation as a student in the Department of Political Science at the University of Wisconsin. That work was done under the supervision of Professor David Fellman, whose help and encouragement, then and later, I acknowledge with great appreciation.

Tucson, Arizona
June 1969   R.C.C.

---

* Richard C. Cortner, *The Wagner Act Cases* (Knoxville: University of Tennessee Press, 1964) .

✥ Contents ঔ

THE JONES & LAUGHLIN CASE

CONSTITUTIONAL DEVELOPMENT ON THE EVE OF THE NEW DEAL

It was clear to both the friends and foes of the government that was established by the Constitution of the United States that a fundamental shift in power from the states to the federal government had occurred. The precise dividing line, however, between those powers delegated to the federal government by which it could regulate in the national interest and those powers remaining in the possession of the states was in many instances left ambiguous by the Constitution. The result has been that the political battles over the enactment of regulatory policies at both the state and federal levels have been transformed into court battles over the constitutional power of the states or the federal government to enact such policies.

THE COMMERCE CLAUSE AND THE STATES

The constitutional battles that have arisen under the Commerce Clause of the Constitution have epitomized the ill-defined constitutional boundaries between federal and state power. The Commerce Clause delegates to the Congress the power to regulate interstate and foreign commerce. Almost immediately after the Constitution's ratification debate began as to the meaning of this clause in regard to the scope of both federal and state power over commerce. Those favoring strong federal control, including the exclusion of state regulation of commerce, argued that the Constitution's delegation of power to Congress to regulate commerce gave Congress exclusive power in that field, and that all state regulation was thus prohibited. Supporters of state control and of state regulation of commerce argued that the power to regulate commerce was shared concurrently by the states and Congress, and that the states could continue to regulate commerce in the absence of conflicting federal legislation on the same subject. Still others supporting state control argued that a reasonably definite line could be drawn delineating those fields of commerce regulable by the states and those regulable by Congress, with each forbidden to enter a field reserved to the other.

In the classic case of Gibbons v. Ogden, 9 Wheat. 1 (1824), Chief Justice John Marshall defined congressional power under the Commerce Clause in classically broad terms. The power of Congress to regulate interstate commerce, Marshall said, was the power to:

> . . . prescribe the rule by which commerce is to be governed. This power, like all others vested in congress, is complete of itself, may be exercised to its utmost extent, and acknowledges no limitations, other than are prescribed in the constitution. . . . The power over commerce with foreign nations, and among the several states, is vested in congress as absolutely as it would be in a single government, having in its constitution the same restrictions on the exercise of the power as are found in the constitution of the United States.

The effect of Marshall's broad definition of congressional power in *Gibbons* v. *Ogden* (1824) was to cast doubt upon the power of the states to regulate commerce in any but very narrow and circumscribed terms. Since the Congress did not exercise the broad power marked out by Marshall until near the end of the nineteenth century, this would have had the effect of exempting most aspects of commerce from any regulation at all. The Taney Court, however, in Cooley v. Board of Wardens, 12 Howard 299 (1852), relaxed the constitutional restraints imposed upon state regulation of commerce by the Marshall Court. While holding in the *Cooley* case that there were areas of commerce which could only be regulated by Congress, the Court also held that there were other areas of commerce which could be regulated by the states in the absence of conflicting congressional legislation. In the latter areas of commerce, therefore, the states were constitutionally free to regulate until Congress chose to exercise its power under the Commerce Clause.

THE EMERGENCE OF NATIONAL REGULATION OF COMMERCE

The Supreme Court helped initiate the modern use of congressional power under the Commerce Clause with its decision in Wabash Railroad v. Illinois, 118 U.S. 557 (1886). In the *Wabash Railroad* case, the Court held that the states could not validly regulate the rates charged by the railroads for the transportation of passengers and goods in interstate commerce. Interstate railroad rates, the Court held, required uniform national regulation, if regulated at all, and therefore such rates fell into that category of commerce within the exclusive preserve of Congress. The result of the decision in the *Wabash Railroad* case was to transfer the political pressure, originally generated at the state level by the Granger movement, for the regulation of railroad rates from the states to the Congress. The congressional response was the passage of the Interstate Commerce Act of 1887, establishing the Interstate Commerce

Commission with limited power, later to be greatly expanded, to regulate interstate railroad rates.

From the time of the *Gibbons* v. *Ogden* (1824) decision to the passing of the Interstate Commerce Act of 1887, most cases coming to the Supreme Court under the Commerce Clause had involved the scope of state power over commerce, since the commerce power of Congress had been relatively unused. After the Interstate Commerce Act, the Sherman Anti-Trust Act of 1890 was passed and an ever increasing volume of congressional legislation was enacted under the Commerce Clause. The Court was thus confronted for the first time with determining in numerous cases the scope of congressional power under the Commerce Clause. In the cases that arose during the nineteenth century that tested the scope of state power over interstate commerce the Court had developed the "direct-indirect effects" formula and the doctrine of "dual federalism" that it now applied when confronted with the issue of the scope of congressional power over commerce at the turn of the century.

Judicial Restrictions on the Commerce Power

The direct-indirect effects formula grew out of cases in which state regulations or taxes were being challenged on the grounds that they constituted attempts at regulation of interstate commerce and were thus in conflict with the power of Congress under the Commerce Clause. In such cases, the Court would often examine the nature of the activity or transaction that was being regulated or taxed by the state, and would attempt to determine whether or not such an activity or transaction affected interstate commerce "directly" or "indirectly." If the Court concluded that the activity being regulated or taxed by the state affected commerce directly, it would hold that such an activity or transaction could only be regulated by Congress and that the state regulation or tax was invalid. On the other hand, if in the Court's opinion an activity or transaction affected commerce only indirectly, then state regulation or taxation of the activity or transaction would be sustained.

The doctrine of dual federalism was also utilized to draw a line between what could be regulated by Congress under the Commerce Clause, and what could legitimately be regulated by the states. This doctrine was based upon the premise that certain activities were reserved to the states for regulation by the Tenth Amendment. Under the doctrine of dual federalism, therefore, the Court considered the reserved powers of the states under the Tenth Amendment to impose an independent limitation upon the powers of the federal government, including the commerce power. The Court held that an attempt on the part of Congress, under the Commerce Clause or through one of its other delegated powers, to regulate in a field reserved to the states violated the Tenth Amendment and was thus invalid.

Both the direct-indirect effects formula and the doctrine of dual federalism emerged in cases involving the scope of state power to regulate and tax interstate commerce. By the end of the nineteenth century, the Court had in such cases also established the doctrine that the production or manufacturing of goods and commodities was not interstate commerce but rather something which affected commerce only indirectly and was reserved to the states for regulation by the Tenth Amendment. Manufacturing, mining, the growing of crops, and other forms of production were considered by the Court to be "local" in nature and thus separate and distinct from interstate commerce. Such activities, the Court reasoned, preceded the movement of goods in interstate commerce and were thus beyond the scope of congressional power under the Commerce Clause.

When at the turn of the century the Court was faced with important cases challenging congressional legislation under the Commerce Clause, it applied the direct-indirect effects formula and the doctrine of dual federalism as tests of the scope of congressional power. One of the first modern uses of the congressional commerce power was the Sherman Anti-Trust Act of 1890. The Sherman Act was a regulation of interstate commerce that prohibited conspiracies, contracts, combinations, or agreements that had the effect of restraining interstate trade. One of the earliest prosecutions by the federal government under the Sherman Act was against the Sugar Trust. One combination of companies had obtained control of 98 percent of the sugar refining capacity in the United States, a condition the government contended was monopolistic and restrictive of interstate trade. When the Sugar Trust case (United States v. E. C. Knight Co., 156 U.S. 1 [1895]), reached the Supreme Court, however, the Court held that the Sherman Act could not be applied to the refining (or manufacture) of sugar because such an activity was not interstate commerce.

Chief Justice Fuller, writing for the Court, said that:

> . . . the power to control the manufacture of a given thing involves in a certain sense the control of its disposition, but this is a secondary and not the primary sense; and although the exercise of that power may result in bringing the operation of commerce into play, it does not control it, and affects it only incidentally and indirectly. Commerce succeeds to manufacture, and is not a part of it.

The doctrine that manufacturing was not commerce, and thus was beyond the power of Congress under the Commerce Clause, Fuller indicated, was necessary to the preservation of a line between congressional power and the power of the states. Such a line was thus believed by the Court to be necessary to the preservation of the federal system:

> It is vital that the independence of the commercial power and of the police power, and the delimitation between them, however sometimes perplexing, should always be recognized and observed,

for while the one furnishes the strongest bond of union, the other is essential to the preservation of the autonomy of the States as required by our dual form of government; and acknowledged evils, however grave and urgent they may appear to be, had better be borne, than the risk be run, in the effort to suppress them, of more serious consequences by resort to expedients of even doubtful constitutionality.

. . . The regulation of commerce applies to the subjects of commerce and not to matters of internal police. Contracts to buy, sell, or exchange goods to be transported among the several States, the transportation and its instrumentalities, and articles bought, sold, or exchanged for the purposes of such transit among the States, or put in the way of transit, may be regulated, but this is because they form part of interstate trade or commerce. The fact that an article is manufactured for export to another State does not of itself make it an article of interstate commerce, and the intent of the manufacturer does not determine the time when the article or product passes from the control of the State and belongs to commerce. . . .

In the Sugar Trust case (1895), the Court therefore converted the direct-indirect effects formula into a test of the scope of congressional power under the Commerce Clause. An activity which affected commerce directly, the Court indicated, could be regulated by Congress; an activity affecting commerce only indirectly, such as manufacturing or production generally, could not be regulated by Congress under the Commerce Clause.

The doctrine of dual federalism, like the direct-indirect effects formula, was also ultimately utilized by the Court to limit the scope of congressional power under the Commerce Clause. In 1916, Congress attempted to outlaw child labor by prohibiting the shipment in interstate commerce of goods produced by child labor. When the Child Labor Act was challenged before the Court in Hammer v. Dagenhart, 247 U.S. 251 (1918), however, it was invalidated on the grounds that congressional power under the Commerce Clause could not be utilized to regulate production industries. Goods produced

by child labor, the Court held, were not in themselves harmful, and when:

> . . . offered for shipment, and before transportation begins, the
> labor of their production is over, and the mere fact that they were
> intended for interstate commerce transportation does not make
> their production subject to federal control under the commerce
> power. . . . The making of goods and the mining of coal are not
> commerce, nor does the fact that these things are to be afterwards
> shipped, or used in interstate commerce, make their production a
> part thereof. . . . Over interstate transportation or its incidents,
> the regulatory power of Congress is ample, but the production of
> articles intended for interstate commerce is a matter of local
> regulation.

The Court then proceeded to state the doctrine of dual federalism in classic form:

> The grant of power to Congress over the subject of interstate
> commerce was to enable it to regulate such commerce, and not to
> give it authority to control the states in their exercise of the police
> power over local trade and manufacture.
>
> The grant of authority over a purely Federal matter was not
> intended to destroy the local power always existing and carefully
> reserved to the states in the 10th Amendment to the Constitution.
>
> * * *
>
> In our view the necessary effect of this act is, by means of a
> prohibition against the movement in interstate commerce of ordi-
> nary commercial commodities, to regulate the hours of labor of
> children in factories and mines within the states,—a purely state
> authority. Thus the act in a twofold sense is repugnant to the
> Constitution. It not only transcends the authority delegated to
> Congress over commerce, but also exerts a power as to a purely
> local matter to which the Federal authority does not extend. The
> far-reaching result of upholding the act cannot be more plainly
> indicated than by pointing out that if Congress can thus regulate
> matters intrusted to local authority by prohibition of the move-
> ment of commodities in interstate commerce, all freedom of com-
> merce will be at an end, and the power of the states over local
> matters may be eliminated, and thus our system of government be
> practically destroyed.

The narrow conception of the commerce power that the Court evidenced in the Sugar Trust (1895) and Child Labor (1918) cases was joined with the due process doctrine of liberty of contract in Adair v. United States, 208 U.S. 161 (1908), to form an important stumbling block to governmental regulation of labor relations. In the *Adair* case, the Court invalidated a congressional attempt to outlaw yellow-dog contracts as a condition of employment on interstate railroads. The yellow-dog contract, as it was labeled by union workers, required a prospective employee to agree not to join a union, or sever his union membership, as a condition of employment. Congress attempted to outlaw such contracts in railroad labor relations in the Erdman Act of 1898. The Court held, however, that labor relations was a subject matter which affected commerce only indirectly and hence lay beyond congressional power under the Commerce Clause. The Court thus noted in the *Adair* case that past decisions had upheld regulations enacted by Congress having "direct reference to the conduct of interstate commerce," but it concluded that "there is no such connection between interstate commerce and membership in a labor organization as to authorize Congress to make it a crime against the United States for an agent of an interstate carrier to discharge an employee because of such membership on his part."

The Court also relied in the *Adair* case (1908) on the doctrine of liberty of contract (a right protected by the Due Process Clauses of the Fifth and Fourteenth Amendments) as a basis for invalidating the anti-yellow-dog contract provision of the Erdman Act. Liberty of contract, a right whose theoretical origins lay in the laissez faire theories of Adam Smith and Herbert Spencer, was accepted by the courts as a fundamental right of property during the latter part of the nineteenth century and was utilized to invalidate a host of socioeconomic legislation. In the *Adair* case, the Court thus held that the Erdman Act's anti-yellow-dog contract provision interfered unreasonably with the right of employers and employees to contract freely in regard to the terms and conditions of employment. The Court held that the:

> . . . right of the employee to quit the service of the employer, for whatever reason, is the same as the right of the employer, for whatever reason, to dispense with the services of such employee. . . . In all such particulars, the employer and the employee have equality of right, and any legislation that disturbs that equality is an arbitrary interference with liberty of contract which no government can legally justify in a free land.

The *Adair* case (1908) thus appeared to prohibit federal legislation that protected the right of workers to belong to labor unions, not only on the grounds that such legislation exceeded the commerce power by reaching activities affecting commerce only indirectly, but also because it interfered with liberty of contract between employers and employees. And in Coppage v. Kansas, 236 U.S. 1 (1915), the Court followed the *Adair* case in invalidating a state statute prohibiting yellow-dog contracts on liberty of contract grounds. By the eve of the New Deal, however, other decisions of the Court had cast doubts upon both the Commerce Clause and the liberty of contract principles of the *Adair* case, as well as the Sugar Trust (1895) and Child Labor (1918) cases.

The Court's conception of interstate commerce which emerged from such decisions as those in the *Adair* (1908), Sugar Trust (1895), and Child Labor (1918) cases was one which perceived interstate commerce as involving primarily interstate transportation and transactions. Production, that is, manufacturing, mining, the growing of crops, and so on, involved essentially local activities which preceded interstate commerce, since the goods produced did not enter interstate commerce until production had ended and they were delivered to a common carrier for shipment out of the state. The power of Congress to regulate interstate commerce could not, therefore, be utilized to reach production enterprises. Under the doctrine of dual federalism, production was a subject matter reserved for regulation by the states under the Tenth Amendment. Production was also classified under the direct-indirect effects formula as an activity that affected interstate commerce indirectly, and congressional power to regulate commerce could be used to reach only those activities which affected commerce directly. The Court's purpose in deciding cases along these lines was obviously to draw a fairly rigid line between state and federal power over economic activity, and to create constitutional compartments within which those matters that could be regulated by the states and those that could be regulated by the Congress could be isolated.

Broad Interpretation of the Commerce Power

The Court, however, developed lines of precedent under the Commerce Clause that to an extent conflicted with its decisions in the Sugar Trust (1895), *Adair* (1908), and Child Labor (1918) cases. Despite its initially narrow interpretation of the Sherman Anti-Trust Act in cases such as the Sugar Trust case, for example, the Court early sustained applications of the act to strikes and boycotts by labor unions which had as their intent a reduction in the flow of particular goods in interstate commerce. The Court's acceptance of the application of the antitrust acts to labor was a major source of the hostility with which organized labor viewed the federal courts. In its application of the antitrust acts to labor, the Court also expanded the scope of congressional power under the Commerce Clause beyond the doctrines of such cases as the Sugar Trust case. While, as we have seen, the Court normally regarded production, such as mining, as an activity beyond the scope of the commerce power, in the *Coronado Coal Company* cases decided in the 1920s,* the Court ultimately sustained the appli-

* United Mine Workers v. Coronado Coal Co., 259 U.S. 344 (1922); and Coronado Coal Co. v. United Mine Workers, 268 U.S. 295 (1925). In

cation of the antitrust acts to a strike in the coal mining industry. Discussing the question of whether the antitrust acts, as
regulations enacted under the Commerce Clause, could be applied to a strike in the coal mines, Chief Justice Taft held:

> . . . coal mining is not interstate commerce, and obstruction of
> coal mining, though it may prevent coal from going into interstate
> commerce, is not a restraint of that commerce unless the obstruc-
> tion of coal mining is intended to restrain commerce in it, or has
> necessarily such a direct, material and substantial effect to restrain
> it that the intent reasonably must be inferred.

From the *Coronado Coal Company* cases (1922, 1925),
therefore, it appeared that production, such as mining, could
be reached by Congress under the Commerce Clause if such
production were obstructed by a strike or some other means
which intended to obstruct commerce in the goods being produced or if the obstruction had a direct, material, and substantial effect on interstate commerce. The Court appeared to say
that Congress in such circumstances could regulate production
for the purpose of removing or prohibiting such obstructions
to interstate commerce.

The Court also acknowledged the power of Congress to regulate essentially "local" activities under the Commerce
Clause in a series of cases which we shall call the "stream of
commerce" cases. Only ten years after its restrictive interpretation of the Commerce Clause in the Sugar Trust case
(1895), the Court decided Swift & Co. v. United States, 196
U.S. 375 (1905). In that case a much more liberal conception
of the power of Congress to regulate commerce was evident.
Like the Sugar Trust case, the *Swift* case involved a prosecution by the government under the Sherman Anti-Trust Act.
In the *Swift* case, the government prosecuted a combination of
the major meat packers controlling approximately 60 percent
of the supply of fresh meat in the country. The meat packers

---

the first case, the Court held the antitrust acts to be inapplicable, but
this conclusion was reversed in the second case.

had agreed that their agents, who purchased livestock at the major stockyards across the country, would not bid against one another. This agreement tended to fix the price at which cattle were sold at the stockyards. They also agreed to bid up the price of livestock from time to time, inducing farmers to ship their livestock to the stockyards for sale. The meat packers would then allow prices to fall to lower levels. The combination of meat packers also fixed the prices at which they would sell fresh meat on the market, and entered into agreements with the railroads by which they paid less than the lawful rates for shipping fresh meat by rail. The government charged that all of these elements of the combination tended to restrain or eliminate competition in interstate commerce in violation of the Sherman Act.

The meat packers argued, however, that when livestock was shipped from farms to the stockyards, such shipment constituted interstate commerce, but the transactions in the stockyards—the bidding, buying, and selling—were local activities which occurred after interstate commerce had ceased. Also, they argued, the sales of fresh meat by them occurred locally, after which the meat was shipped to the buyers. The agreements entered into by the packers, it was argued, related to local activities and not to interstate commerce, and were therefore beyond the reach of Congress under the Commerce Clause and the Sherman Act.

Justice Holmes, writing for a unanimous Court in the *Swift* case (1905), rejected these contentions and declared that:

> . . . commerce among the states is not a technical legal conception, but a practical one, drawn from the course of business. When cattle are sent for sale from a place in one state, with the expectation that they will end their transit, after purchase, in another, and when in effect they do so, with only the interruption necessary to find a purchaser at the stock yards, and when this is a typical, constantly recurring course, the current thus existing is a current of commerce among the states, and the purchase of the cattle is a part and incident of such commerce.

Although the combination by the meat packers, Holmes said, involved "restraint and monopoly of trade within a single state, its effect upon commerce among the states is not accidental, secondary, remote, or merely probable," and it was therefore prohibited by the Sherman Act.

The Court's decision in the *Swift* case (1905) rejected the conception of commerce as being primarily transportation which had emerged from the Sugar Trust case (1895). Interstate commerce, in the *Swift* case, was considered to be broader than transportation and to embrace interstate trade generally. And local activities which occurred as part of a recurring "current" or "stream" of interstate trade, or affected such trade substantially, could be regulated by Congress under the Commerce Clause, even though those local incidents when viewed in isolation were not themselves interstate commerce. In contrast with the direct-indirect effects formula and the doctrine of dual federalism, interstate commerce in the *Swift* case was thus viewed by the Court, as Holmes said, not as a "technical legal conception, but a practical one, drawn from the course of business."

The *Swift* case (1905) was heavily relied upon by the Court in the early 1920s to uphold the Packers and Stockyards Act of 1921 and the Grain Futures Act of 1922. The Packers and Stockyards Act outlawed various deceptive practices used by those engaged in the buying and selling of livestock in the stockyards and also regulated the rates which commission men, the middlemen in the buying and selling process, could charge for their services. As in the *Swift* case, the commission men, meat packers, and others regulated by the act argued that their activities in the stockyards were local activities and not interstate commerce, since the buying and selling of livestock at the stockyards occurred after the livestock's interstate shipment had ceased. Chief Justice Taft, writing for the Court in Stafford v. Wallace, 258 U.S. 495 (1922), nonetheless sustained the validity of the Packers and Stockyards Act on the basis of the *Swift* case. "The application of the commerce clause of the Constitution in the Swift Case," Taft said, "was the result of the natural development of interstate commerce under modern conditions. It was the inevitable result of the great central fact that such streams of commerce from one part of the country to another which are ever flowing are in their very essence the commerce among the States. . . ." Although when viewed in isolation, the buying and selling of livestock at stockyards might appear to be local, the Court nevertheless held that whatever:

> . . . amounts to more or less constant practice, and threatens to obstruct or unduly to burden the freedom of interstate commerce, is within the regulatory power of Congress under the commerce clause, and it is primarily for Congress to consider and decide the fact of the danger and meet it. This Court will certainly not substitute its judgment for that of Congress in such a matter unless the relation of the subject to interstate commerce and its effect upon it are clearly non-existent.

The *Swift* case (1905) was again relied upon by the Court to sustain the Grain Futures Act in Chicago Board of Trade v. Olsen, 262 U.S. 1 (1923). In the Grain Futures Act, the Congress was regulating manipulations in the grain futures market, activities which occurred locally but which affected the prices at which grain sold in the interstate markets. The Court again cited the *Swift* case as having "recognized the great changes and development in the business of this vast country," and as having "refused to permit local incidents of great interstate movement, which, taken alone, were intrastate, to characterize the movement as such. . . ." The Swift case "merely fitted the commerce clause to the real and practical essence of modern business growth. It applies to the case before us just as it did in Stafford v. Wallace." The Court refused to question the conclusion of Congress that the manipulation "of the market for futures on the Chicago Board of Trade may, and from time to time does, directly burden and obstruct commerce between the States in grain, and that it recurs and is a constantly possible danger. For this reason Congress has the power to provide the appropriate means adopted in this Act by which this abuse may be restrained and avoided."

In the *Swift* (1905), *Stafford* (1922), and *Olsen* (1923) cases, the Court had thus provided a line of precedent which supported a much broader conception of the power of Congress under the Commerce Clause than the Sugar Trust (1895), *Adair* (1908), and Child Labor (1918) cases. In the stream of commerce cases, the Court had held that commerce embraced not only interstate transportation but also commercial trade of all kinds. And the power of Congress extended not only to the regulation and control of interstate transportation and trade, but to those local activities which burdened, obstructed, or interfered with commerce. The stream of commerce cases were therefore the most important line of cases decided by the Court that supported a broad interpretation of congressional power under the Commerce Clause until the 1930s, and they were heavily relied upon when New Deal measures were defended before the Court.

The Railroad Cases

Another line of cases, however, also supported a rather broad construction of congressional power under the Commerce Clause. These were the railroad cases in which the Court sustained various measures enacted by Congress to regulate interstate railroads. In 1907, for example, Congress enacted the Hours of Service Act prohibiting those responsible for the movement of interstate trains from being employed for more than eight hours per day. Challenging the statute, the railroads argued that their employees were employed in the movement of trains in both interstate and intrastate commerce, and that the act was therefore invalid because it reached intrastate matters that were beyond the power of Congress to regulate. The Court, however, upheld the act in the Hours of Service Case (Baltimore & Ohio Railroad Co. v. I.C.C., 221 U.S. 612 [1911]), pointing out that the power of Congress to protect interstate commerce could not be frustrated by the fact that persons performing tasks related to the interstate movement of trains also performed work relating to intrastate commerce. If, in order to effectively protect interstate commerce, the Court held, Congress had to reach activities which were intrastate in nature, then it was not beyond the power of Congress to regulate such intrastate activities.

The Court reached a similar conclusion in the Safety Appliance Case (Southern Railroad Co. v. United States, 222 U.S. 20 [1911]). In the Safety Appliance Act of 1903, Congress had directed that all trains, whether engaged in interstate commerce or intrastate commerce, should be equipped with safety devices. The Court again rejected an argument that such a regulation was invalid because it reached purely intrastate commerce. The Court pointed out that the safety of interstate trains would be jeopardized if intrastate trains were not also required to have safety devices. Congressional power over interstate commerce, the Court said, was "plenary, and competently may be exerted to secure the safety of persons and property transported therein and of those who are employed in such transportation, no matter what may be the source of the dangers that threaten it." In 1912, the Federal Employers' Liability Act, which established a workmen's compensation system on interstate railroads, was similarly upheld as a valid regulation of commerce in the Second Employers' Liability Act case (Mondou v. New York, N.H. & H. Ry. Co., 223 U.S. 1). And in Wilson v. New, 243 U.S. 332 (1917), the Court upheld the power of Congress under the Commerce Clause to prescribe working conditions on interstate railroads temporarily in order to avoid a nationwide rail strike.

In 1914, the Court in addition upheld the power of the Interstate Commerce Commission to require that the intrastate rates charged by the railroads conform to interstate rates, so that discrimination against interstate commerce would not occur. Justice Hughes, writing for the Court in the Shreveport case (Houston, East & West Texas Railroad Co. v. United States, 234 U.S. 342 [1914]), provided a good summary of the scope of congressional power recognized by the Court in the railroad cases:

> While these decisions sustaining the Federal power relate to measures adopted in the interest of the safety of persons and property, they illustrate the principle that Congress, in the exercise of its paramount power, may prevent the common instrumentalities of interstate and intrastate commercial intercourse from being used in their intrastate operations to the injury of interstate commerce. This is not to say that Congress possesses the authority to regulate the internal commerce of a state, as such, but that it does possess the power to foster and protect interstate commerce, and to take all measures necessary or appropriate to that end, although intrastate transactions of interstate carriers may thereby be controlled.

As in the stream of commerce cases, the Court had enunciated principles in the railroad cases that recognized that Congress could reach essentially local activities under the Commerce Clause when their regulation was necessary or appropriate to the effective regulation of interstate commerce. The principles that emerged from the railroad and stream of commerce cases thus contrasted sharply with the rather rigid compartmentalization of interstate and local activities that constituted the Court's conception of commerce under the direct-indirect effects formula and the doctrine of dual federalism. On the eve of the New Deal, in the field of interstate commerce, therefore, the Court possessed alternative and rather conflicting lines of precedent, which could be utilized to sustain or invalidate exercises of power by Congress in regulating the economy. This ambiguity of constitutional doctrine was heightened by the Court's decision in Texas & New

Orleans Railroad Co. v. Brotherhood of Railway and Steamship Clerks, 281 U.S. 548 (1930).

As we have seen in the *Adair* case (1908), the Court had held that the Erdman Act's prohibition of yellow-dog contracts was an invalid interference with liberty of contract under the Fifth Amendment. The Court had also held in the *Adair* case that labor relations were local in nature and therefore beyond the reach of Congress under the Commerce Clause. In 1926, however, Congress enacted the Railway Labor Act which provided for the mediation of labor disputes on interstate railroads and prohibited the railroads from interfering with the right of their employees to belong to labor unions. The Texas & New Orleans Railroad had fired several of its employees who belonged to a union, but a federal district court held this to violate the Railway Labor Act and ordered the railroad to restore the employees to their jobs.

The Railway Labor Act and the district court's order enforcing it thus clearly appeared to be invalid under the principles of *Adair* v. *United States* (1908), but when the railroad appealed to the Supreme Court, the Court upheld the validity of the act. Writing for the Court, Chief Justice Hughes held that there was "no doubt of the constitutional authority of Congress to enact the prohibition." Exercising its power under the Commerce Clause, Hughes said, "Congress may facilitate the amicable settlement of disputes which threaten the necessary agencies of transportation." The right of employees to organize into unions, the Chief Justice continued, had long been recognized:

Congress was not required to ignore this right of the employees but [could] safeguard it and seek to make appropriate collective action an instrument of peace rather than strife. Such collective action would be a mockery if representation were made futile by interferences with freedom of choice. Thus the prohibition by Congress of interference with the selection of representatives for the purpose of negotiation and conference between employers and employees, instead of being an invasion of the constitutional rights of either, was based on the recognition of the rights of both.

In regard to the liberty of contract objections to the act, the Court merely held that the *Adair* case (1908) was "inapplicable." The Court said:

> The Railway Labor Act of 1926 does not interfere with the normal exercise of the right of the carrier to select its employees or to discharge them. The statute is not aimed at this right of employers, but at interference with the right of employees to have representatives of their own choosing. As the carriers subject to the act have no constitutional right to interfere with the freedom of the employees in making their selections, they cannot complain of the statute on constitutional grounds.

The *Texas & New Orleans Railroad* case (1930) thus constituted another precedent for the broad exercise of congressional power under the Commerce Clause, a precedent that to an extent again conflicted with the principles of cases in which the Court had taken a more restrictive position in regard to the commerce power. The *Texas & New Orleans Railroad* case additionally left such cases as *Adair* v. *United States* (1908) and *Coppage* v. *Kansas* (1915) in a state of limbo. Could Congress or the states protect the right to organize into unions generally without invalidly interfering with liberty of contract? And could Congress regulate labor relations affecting commerce generally under the Commerce Clause, or were they still regarded as "local" activities as the *Adair* case had implied? The Court had simply held the principles of the *Adair* and *Coppage* cases to be "inapplicable" in the *Texas & New Orleans Railroad* case without reversing those cases, and as a result their status as precedent was murky after 1930.

THE SUPREME COURT ON THE EVE OF THE NEW DEAL

This uncertainty as to the scope of congressional power over labor relations and the economy was generally increased by significant changes in the membership of the Supreme Court between 1930 and 1932. Throughout the 1920s, the Court had been dominated by a solid conservative majority composed of Chief Justice Taft and Justices Sanford, Sutherland, Butler, Van Devanter, and McReynolds, while Justices Holmes, Brandeis, and Stone were frequent dissenters from the majority decisions of the Court. Chief Justice Taft and Justice Sanford both left the Court in 1930 and Charles Evans Hughes was appointed as Taft's replacement. President Hoover nominated Court of Appeals Judge John J. Parker to replace Sanford, but the National Association for the Advancement of Colored People and the American Federation of Labor attacked Parker on the grounds he was anti-Negro and anti-labor. The AFL particularly pointed to a decision Parker had made on the Court of Appeals in which he had enforced yellow-dog contracts. Senate progressives joined the AFL and the NAACP in the attack upon Parker. Debate on Parker's nomination was taking place during the time the *Texas & New Orleans Railroad* case (1930) was pending before the Court. Senator Borah, attacking Parker's yellow-dog contract decision, thus pointed out that the issue was before the Court again and that:

> . . . it is possible that Judge Parker would be permitted to sit in that case and help determine it before it is finally decided. . . . I would not myself vote to put a man upon the Supreme Court who is committed to the doctrine, regardless of how he became committed. I think this is so fundamental, so righteous in and of itself that I could not get my consent to put upon the Supreme Court a man who had already declared his position upon the question. The court is divided; the controversy is there again. . . .

The Senate rejected Parker by a vote of thirty-nine to forty-one, the first time in the twentieth century a presidential nominee to the Supreme Court had been rejected by the Senate. President Hoover then nominated Owen J. Roberts, and he was quickly confirmed by the Senate. Finally, in 1932 Justice

Holmes retired from the Court, and President Hoover appointed Benjamin Cardozo of the New York Court of Appeals as his replacement. As a result of these changes on the Court, the solid conservative majority of the 1920s had been reduced to Justices Sutherland, Van Devanter, Butler, and McReynolds. Cardozo was commonly regarded as a liberal and was expected to align himself with Justices Brandeis and Stone. The key men on the Court were therefore Chief Justice Hughes and Justice Roberts, since one or both of their votes would give a majority to either the liberal or conservative blocs on the Court.

In addition to the uncertainty created by the conflicting lines of precedent in regard to congressional power over the economy, on the eve of the New Deal there also existed uncertainty as to how the Justices would align themselves on major constitutional issues. If nothing else, however, the rejection of Parker in 1930 should have served as a warning to the Court that there was powerful opposition to the conservative course of constitutional development that it had been following. And as the depression deepened and the election of 1932 brought Franklin D. Roosevelt to the presidency, it could be expected that the opposition manifested in the Senate on the Parker nomination would be growing in strength not only in the Congress but in the country at large.

❦ 2 ❧

THE NEW DEAL COMES
TO "LITTLE SIBERIA"

————◆————

Twenty-six miles below Pittsburgh, along the Ohio River, is an area that in 1907 was called Woodlawn Park. The area had obvious advantages as a location for manufacturing steel. It was centrally located in relation to the Pennsylvania and West Virginia coal and limestone deposits and the great iron ore deposits of Michigan and Minnesota. The essentials for manufacturing steel could thus be easily transported by barge on the Ohio River to the Woodlawn Park area where they could be transformed into steel to meet the steadily increasing national demand.

The advantages of the Woodlawn Park area for manufacturing steel were recognized early by the Jones & Laughlin Steel Corporation. Jones & Laughlin was founded by B. F. Jones, who had started with a small rolling mill in Brownsville, Pennsylvania, and had later moved his operation to Pittsburgh. The company was reorganized and incorporated in 1902, and in 1907, recognizing the advantages of the Woodlawn Park area, the company purchased it. The name of the area was later changed to Aliquippa.

"LITTLE SIBERIA"

At Aliquippa, Jones & Laughlin built a company town and a plant for the production of steel. Aliquippa became a paternalistically administered company town similar to other company towns that could be found in the coal fields and the cotton mill areas of the country. Aliquippa was laid out in sections, with each section containing the homes of the different racial and national groups that made up Jones & Laughlin's employees. The groups included Italians, Poles, Serbians, Greeks, Russians, and Negroes. In 1914 Jones & Laughlin hired Tom M. Girdler as assistant superintendent of the Aliquippa works and instructed him to make Aliquippa "the best steel town in the world. We want to make it the best possible place for a steel-worker to raise a family." Girdler hired Harry Mauk, an ex-state policeman, to head the company police, and proceeded to create in Aliquippa what he later admitted was a "benevolent dictatorship."

Jones & Laughlin had eliminated unionism among its employees in 1897 following the disastrous Homestead strike in 1892 against the Carnegie Steel Company. The Homestead strike had resulted in a pitched battle between the strikers and a force of Pinkerton operatives hired by the Carnegie Company. The attempted assassination of Henry C. Frick, the president of the Carnegie Company, and the breaking of the Homestead strike by the state militia began a drive against unionism in the steel industry, and Jones & Laughlin followed this trend. The most ambitious attempt to unionize the steel industry following the Homestead strike came in 1919 when approximately four hundred thousand steel workers struck seeking union recognition, higher wages, and the eight hour day. The 1919 strike collapsed in the atmosphere of a public opinion that was rapidly moving toward conservatism in the wake of World War I, and the Red hysteria which characterized the period. It is perhaps indicative of the efficiency of the company police system in rooting out unionism and the "benevolent dictatorship" established at Aliquippa by Tom Girdler that Jones & Laughlin did not lose a single man-hour due to the 1919 strike.

By the 1930s, Aliquippa was known to union organizers as "Little Siberia" because of the stringency of the enforcement there of Jones & Laughlin's policy against unions. The company's grip on the community was indeed formidable. The company owned 674 of its employees' homes as well as the city transportation facilities and the city water company. Employees were thus dependent upon the company in many instances for housing, transportation, and water, in addition to employment.

Jones & Laughlin's economic dominance of the community was matched by its political dominance. Beaver County, in which Aliquippa was located, was dominated politically by former state senator David Craig who reportedly was retained by Jones & Laughlin as an attorney. The sheriff of Beaver County was Charles O'Laughlin, a former Aliquippa police officer. The Aliquippa Chief of Police was W. L. Ambrose, a former Jones & Laughlin company police officer, and the warden of the county jail was a former Aliquippa chief of police. All of the Jones & Laughlin company police also held commissions as special borough policemen.

It is therefore not difficult to understand why the Jones & Laughlin plant at Aliquippa remained unaffected by the strike of 1919 or why Aliquippa was known as "Little Siberia" to union organizers during the 1930s. Through its political and economic domination of the community Jones & Laughlin effectively harassed and intimidated any of its employees who harbored pro-union sentiments as well as union organizers who had the temerity to come to Aliquippa. The company

thus effectively prohibited any open, public union meetings in
Aliquippa until the mid-1930s.

By the time of the New Deal, the Jones & Laughlin Steel
Corporation had moved from its humble beginnings as B. F.
Jones' rolling mill to the position of the fourth largest steel
producer in the United States. The company employed
22,000 workers, 10,000 of them at its Aliquippa plant. The
company owned iron ore, coal, and limestone properties in
Michigan, Minnesota, Pennsylvania, and West Virginia. In
addition it owned railroad and river barge subsidiaries by
which these raw materials were transported to its plants at
Pittsburgh and Aliquippa. The company also owned a nationwide system of subsidiaries for the distribution of its steel
products. Its gross assets were valued at more than 181 million dollars.

BEGINNING OF THE NEW DEAL

Jones & Laughlin, along with industry generally, was se-
verely affected by the stock market crash and ensuing depression that began during the fall of 1929. The inability of the
Hoover administration to cope effectively with the economic
disaster led to its overwhelming defeat at the polls in 1932, the
election of Franklin D. Roosevelt as President, and overwhelmingly Democratic majorities in the Congress. Roosevelt
seemed to offer the voters the possibility of change and the
promise of new methods of dealing with the depression.
What specifically Roosevelt and the Democratic party would
do had been left ambiguous during the campaign, in conform-
ity with the hallowed traditions of American electoral campaigns. As a result of the election it seemed evident that there
was an overwhelming popular demand for action to overcome
the depression and that at least initially there was a great deal
of unity among most groups in the country in support of any
plan that would lead the country back to prosperity.

The principal program that emerged during the famous "hundred days" of the Roosevelt administration for dealing with the problems of industrial recovery was the National Industrial Recovery Act of 1933. The NIRA contemplated a cooperative effort among industrial groups, labor, and the government to bring about economic recovery. To this end the Congress provided in the NIRA that trade associations or industrial groups could draft codes outlawing "unfair competitive practices" that were detrimental to economic conditions within particular industries. These codes, once approved and promulgated by the President, would have the force of law. As a concession to labor the Congress also provided that the codes governing particular industries had to contain provisions setting minimum wages and maximum hours, regulating child labor, and guaranteeing the right of labor to organize. The latter provision was embodied in Section 7 (a) of the NIRA, which stated that:

. . . employees shall have the right to organize and bargain collectively through representatives of their own choosing, and shall be free from the interference, restraint or coercion of employers of labor, or their agents, in the designation of such representatives or in self-organization or in other concerted activities for the purpose of collective bargaining or other mutual aid or protection. . . . no employee and no one seeking employment shall be required as a condition of employment to join any company union or to refrain from joining, organizing, or assisting a labor organization of his own choosing.

Section 7 (a) thus appeared to extend to workers covered by NIRA codes governmental protection of their right to organize into labor unions as well as outlawing the yellow-dog contract. "The President wants you to join a union," John L. Lewis' United Mine Workers alleged in a successful organizing campaign after the passage of NIRA. While union membership generally increased during the existence of NIRA, the promise of Section 7 (a) from the union standpoint was crushed upon the political and economic realities that were concealed for a time behind the façade of unity that surrounded the initiation of the recovery effort.

The NIRA and the Steel Industry

It was soon apparent that those industries that were traditionally anti-union and open shop would attempt to circumvent Section 7 (a) by any means possible. Most employer groups announced early their opposition to Section 7 (a). Robert P. Lamont, speaking for the Iron and Steel Institute which repesented the major steel producers, declared that the steel industry was "opposed to conducting negotiations . . . otherwise than with its own employees; it is unwilling to conduct them with outside organizations of labor or with individuals not its employees."

The Iron and Steel Institute, like many other employer groups, sought to qualify the language of section 7 (a) in the code that it formulated to govern the steel industry under NIRA. The Institute's draft code endorsed company unions and restricted representatives of employees in the steel industry to the employees of the particular steel companies, thus eliminating the chance that steel employees might select as their bargaining representatives "outside" labor union officials. General Hugh Johnson, the Director of the National Recovery Administration (the administrative agency created to administer the provisions of NIRA), objected to the Steel Institute's attempt to qualify Section 7 (a) in this manner. The Institute agreed to withdraw the language from the proposed steel code. The Institute emphasized, however, that its withdrawal of the language qualifying Section 7 (a) in the code did not "imply any change in the attitude of the industry or the parts therein." The steel industry still considered unions to be "of no profit to anyone concerned, unless it be the many racketeers who have fastened themselves on the unions."

Despite the fact that most employer groups, like the Iron and Steel Institute, failed to obtain qualifications of Section 7 (a) in the codes they developed governing their industries, widespread violations of the right to organize guaranteed by Section 7 (a) were soon evident in the recovery effort. Employers established and supported company unions with which to "bargain," seeking to head off the organization of their employees by bona fide labor unions. There was also widespread harassment and intimidation of union organizers and employees seeking to join unions by anti-union employers.

The attitude of anti-unionism in the steel industry was indicated by an incident that occurred during the period in which the steel code under NIRA was being formulated. Secretary of Labor Frances Perkins called in a number of steel executives to meet with William Green, the president of the American Federation of Labor, to discuss the provisions of the proposed steel code. Upon being introduced to Green most of the steel executives backed into a corner of the Secretary's office and refused to shake hands. They were afraid, they said, that the word would get back to the steel towns that they had talked on a friendly basis with Green.

Certainly this attitude of intransigent opposition to unionism was reflected in the actions taken by the Jones & Laughlin Steel Corporation to prevent the unionization of its employees during the NIRA period. In 1933 Jones & Laughlin established a company union following the pattern set by other employers in their attempts to prevent the possibility of the unionization of their employees under Section 7 (a). Jones & Laughlin apparently anticipated the possibility of labor trouble during the NIRA period, and purchased during the period 1933 to 1935 over four thousand dollars worth of tear and sickening gas.

The AFL union possessing jurisdiction over the steel industry was the Amalgamated Association of Iron, Steel and Tin Workers. Its president in 1933 was Michael Tighe, who seemed content to preside over the 4,852 members that Amalgamated had managed to organize and to negotiate the union contracts that Amalgamated had managed to secure with some minor steel firms. Despite prodding from AFL president William Green, Tighe and Amalgamated's executive board did not attempt to push an organizing drive in the steel industry taking advantage of Section 7 (a) of NIRA until late in the summer of 1933. Although this organizing drive did succeed in increasing the membership of Amalgamated to over eighteen thousand by 1934, the drive was ultimately unsuccessful. The failure of the government to effectively protect the right to organize as provided for by Section 7 (a), and the obdurate resistance by the steel companies, prevented any large scale unionization of the steel industry during the NIRA period.

The NIRA in Aliquippa

Jones & Laughlin's response to the threat of unionization was typical of the steel industry. Amalgamated's organizing drive succeeded in inducing several Jones & Laughlin employees to join the union, and a local union affiliated with the Amalgamated was chartered in Aliquippa in August 1934. As a result of this activity a campaign of harassment and intimidation against the union members was begun. Angelo Volpe's home was raided and he was constantly followed by Aliquippa police after he refused an offer from the Jones & Laughlin company police to work for them against the union. Martin Gerstner, another union member, held a union meeting at his home. Company police placed his home under surveillance and threatened the workers who had attended the meeting as they left. Harry V. Phillips, the president of the local union, was assaulted by two men in late August. When he sought protection from the Aliquippa police he was told to get "the hell out of here. You don't deserve protection."

An even more graphic demonstration of the hazards faced

by union members and organizers in Aliquippa came in 1934. Despite the intimidation of the membership, the union hired a former Jones & Laughlin employee, George Isaski, as an organizer for the union during 1934. Isaski was, however, soon arrested on the charge of being drunk and disorderly. He was jailed for thirty days and his wife was refused permission to visit him. While Isaski was serving his sentence the sheriff petitioned the county judge to convene a lunacy commission to examine Isaski to determine his sanity. The judge complied, appointing an attorney known to be rabidly anti-union and two medical doctors, one employed by the county commissioners and the other employed as the jail physician, to constitute a lunacy commission to pass upon Isaski's mental condition. There is no record of any testimony or witnesses heard by the lunacy commission, but on September 19, 1934, Isaski was ordered committed to the Torrence State Hospital for the Insane. Because of the secrecy of the proceedings of the lunacy commission neither Isaski's wife nor his friends were aware of his commitment for a time.

Fortunately for Isaski, the Governor of Pennsylvania at this time was the long-time progressive, Gifford Pinchot, and Isaski's fate finally came to the attention of the Governor's office. Pinchot's wife, Cornelia, wanted to dramatize to the country the tactics being utilized by the steel companies against their employees by dramatically kidnapping Isaski from the mental hospital. The Governor, however, discovered a loophole in the law which allowed him to obtain Isaski's release. This was done after Isaski had been pronounced sane by a state psychologist.

Labor boards were created under the NIRA by many of the codes governing particular industries. Under the Steel Code there was provision for a National Steel Labor Relations Board. Boards such as the NSLRB were responsible for supervising the observance of the labor provisions embodied in the various NIRA codes, and particularly Section 7 (a) of NIRA which guaranteed the right of workers to organize free from employer interference.   The tactics of the Jones & Laughlin Steel Corporation in intimidating union organizers and members at Aliquippa came to the attention of the NSLRB, and the Board scheduled a hearing on the matter in October 1934 to be held in Pittsburgh.   Several union members who were employed by Jones & Laughlin at Aliquippa travelled to Pittsburgh for the NSLRB hearing prepared to testify that Jones & Laughlin was systematically violating Section 7 (a) of the NIRA through its policy of intimidation and harassment of union members and organizers.

The NSLRB hearing, however, was postponed at the last moment.   The union members from Aliquippa then requested from the Board a guarantee of safe conduct and protection upon their return to Aliquippa, indicating that they feared reprisals against them because of their willingness to testify against Jones & Laughlin at the hearing.   This request piqued the interest of the NSLRB with the result that Governor Pinchot was requested to insure the union members' safety by sending state police into Aliquippa.   The Governor dispatched seven state policemen to Aliquippa where they established headquarters at the Woodlawn Hotel.   The presence of the state police resulted in a considerable reduction of tension in Aliquippa and a temporary abatement of Jones & Laughlin's campaign of intimidation against the union.   On October 14, Governor Pinchot's wife Cornelia addressed the first open, public labor meeting ever held in Aliquippa.   The union was also able for the first time to rent space for a headquarters in Aliquippa.

THE FAILURE OF THE NIRA LABOR BOARDS

The Aliquippa episode was one of the successes of the NSLRB, but the labor board system established under the NIRA was generally unable to enforce effectively Section

7 (a). During 1934 the conflict between the steel industry and the union threatened to break out into an industry-wide steel strike. President Roosevelt was forced to intervene in the situation with a proposal that the NSLRB work out a compromise between the industry and labor on the issue of union recognition. During the fall and winter of 1934 negotiations were carried on between the steel industry and the union through the auspices of the NSLRB. The industry agreed that it would meet with any of its employees and seek to adjust grievances, but it refused to agree to sign a contract with the union or to recognize the union as the exclusive bargaining agent for steel employees. The union was demanding representation elections to determine if a majority of steel workers desired the union to represent them and also that the industry recognize the jurisdiction of the NSLRB to hear and act upon instances of anti-union action by the industry. The result of the NSLRB negotiations was a stalemate. The industry would not agree to recognize the union or the jurisdiction of the NSLRB over anti-union complaints. The union would not abandon its demands for representation elections and recognition of the legitimacy of the NSLRB's jurisdiction. Despite pressure from the White House for some kind of compromise settlement in steel, the industry and the union remained deadlocked on the basic issues separating them throughout the NIRA period and therefore Section 7 (a) was far from effectively enforced in the industry.

In addition to the special industry boards, such as the NSLRB, the National Labor Board was also established under the NIRA to enforce the right to organize guaranteed by Section 7 (a). The NLB was composed of employer and labor representatives and was chaired by Senator Robert F. Wagner of New York. Like the special industry boards, the NLB suffered from the fact that the principal goal of NIRA was economic recovery, with the protection of the right to organize as a relatively peripheral issue from the standpoint of the Roose-

velt administration. The NLB was also weakened as an effective enforcer of Section 7 (a) by the lack of effective legal sanc-
tions that could be invoked against violators. If the NLB
determined that an employer was violating Section 7 (a), it
was dependent upon the Compliance Division of the National
Recovery Administration (NRA) to take action against the
employer. The Compliance Division of NRA, however, could
generally only order the employer to cease displaying the blue
eagle, the symbol of compliance with the NIRA, from his business premises or on his products. This sanction had some effect during the early days when there was a great deal of national unity behind the recovery effort but as time went on
and business and public disillusionment with the recovery program became greater, the symbolic power of the blue eagle
also declined.

Other than action by the Compliance Division of NRA, the
NLB could recommend to the Justice Department that an employer in violation of Section 7 (a) be prosecuted. The Justice Department, however, had grave doubts as to the validity
of the NIRA under the Constitution so it pursued a strategy
throughout the NIRA period of avoiding as long as possible
the day of reckoning when the act would have to be defended
before the Supreme Court, a policy which was ultimately to
prove disastrous. In any event, the Justice Department was
reluctant to begin prosecutions against violators of the NIRA
for fear that the federal courts would rule the act invalid.
This was particularly true in regard to suits enforcing Section
7 (a) which was not central to the NIRA's recovery scheme
and was of very doubtful constitutionality.

The NLB was thus almost exclusively dependent upon negotiation and conciliation as methods to enforce Section 7 (a)
and to settle labor disputes within industries. The Board
soon developed the principle that employees should be allowed to vote in representation elections that would allow
them the opportunity to choose labor unions as their repre-

sentatives in bargaining with employers. This principle was vigorously attacked by the National Association of Manufacturers and the Iron and Steel Institute, both of which took the position that employees should be restricted in representation elections to voting for their fellow employees to represent them in negotiations with employers, and that the choice of "outsiders," that is, labor unions, should not be permitted in such elections. The NLB also developed the principle that when a majority of employees of a particular business voted in favor of a particular representative, that representative would be the exclusive representative of all employees in negotiations over working conditions with the employer. Despite general business opposition, the NLB had some success in settling labor disputes on the basis of majority rule and representation election principles.

In 1934, however, the NLB ran into obdurate resistance when it attempted to apply these principles to the Weirton Steel Company. Weirton Steel had at first agreed to a representation election among its employees under the auspices of the NLB, but it later repudiated this agreement. Instead, the company decided to hold an election itself in which its employees would be allowed to vote only on the issue of whether or not they favored a company union established and controlled by Weirton. General Hugh Johnson warned the company that it was "about to commit a deliberate violation of federal law," but to no avail. Senator Wagner, as chairman of the NLB, then requested the Attorney General to initiate a prosecution against the Weirton Steel Company for violation of Section 7 (a).

The Justice Department subsequently sought an injunction against the employee election at Weirton from a federal district court. In meeting the arguments of the company's attorneys that Section 7 (a) was unconstitutional, the Justice Department attorneys argued that Congress could validly regulate the labor relations of Weirton under the Commerce

Clause. Invoking the stream of commerce cases the government thus argued that a labor dispute at the Weirton Steel Company would obstruct and burden the flow or stream of steel products in interstate commerce. The federal district court, however, dismissed these contentions out of hand and refused to issue the injunction. The government's stream of commerce argument, the court said, was "devious." "The manufacturing operations conducted by defendant in its various plants or mills, do not constitute interstate commerce. The relations between defendant and its employees do not affect interstate commerce."

The government had also argued that the right to organize on the part of workers needed protection in order that they could bargain collectively with their employers on roughly equal terms. This argument, the court held, was:

> . . . based on the assumption of an inevitable and necessary diversity of interests [between employees and employers]. This is the traditional old world theory. It is not the Twentieth Century American theory of that relation as dependent upon mutual interest, understanding and good will. This modern theory is embodied in the Weirton plan of employee organization. Furthermore, the suggestion that recurrent hard times suspend constitutional limitations or cause manufacturing operations to so affect interstate commerce as to subject them to regulation by Congress borders on the fantastic and merits no serious consideration.

The court consequently held that Section 7 (a) as applied to the Weirton Steel Company was unconstitutional because it went beyond the power of Congress under the Commerce Clause.*

The National Labor Board had staked its prestige on a successful prosecution of the Weirton Steel Company and the district court's decision was a major blow to any hope that the NLB could be able to enforce Section 7 (a) with any degree of effectiveness. The effect of the *Weirton* case was to reinforce

* United States v. Weirton Steel Co., 10 F. Supp. 55 (D.Del., 1935).

the doubts about the constitutional validity of Section 7 (a) , adding the constitutional issue to the difficulties the NLB was already encountering in enforcing that Section.

The Defeat of the Wagner Bill

As chairman of the NLB, Senator Robert Wagner became painfully aware of the shortcomings of the enforceability of the right of workers to organize under the NIRA. Wagner had come up through the ranks in Charley Murphy's Tammany Hall Democratic organization in New York City. Born in Germany in 1878, Wagner had emigrated with his family to the United States in 1886. In 1904 Wagner had been elected with Tammany support to the New York State legislature, and in 1909 he was elected to the state Senate where he became Democratic majority leader. In 1919 Wagner was elected to the New York Supreme Court but resigned that position to run successfully for the U.S. Senate in 1926. By the time of the New Deal, Wagner was recognized by organized labor as one of its best friends in the Congress. He was convinced that the unequal economic power employers possessed in relation to their employees made economic democracy impossible, and if democracy was to be a viable principle in industry the workers had to be protected in their right to organize and bargain collectively in order to offset the economic power of their employers.

Believing in these principles of industrial democracy, and recognizing the deficiencies in the protection of the right of workers to organize under the NIRA, Senator Wagner introduced a bill in 1934 that outlawed various forms of "unfair labor practices" that employers utilized to interfere with the right to ogranize. The bill also established permanent machinery to replace the temporary labor board system to enforce the right to organize. The prospects for the passage of Wagner's bill by the Congress during 1934 appeared to be good, although employer groups launched a massive attack upon the bill during Senate hearings. James A. Emery, general counsel of the National Association of Manufacturers, argued eloquently that the bill was totally unconstitutional. The Congress could not, Emery said, regulate labor relations in manufacturing or production industries because such businesses were not engaged in interstate commerce. In addition to the bill's invalidity under the Commerce Clause, he argued that in preventing employer interference with the right of workers to organize the bill violated the liberty of contract that was protected by the Due Process Clause of the Fifth Amendment.

In addition to the NAM, numerous representatives of other industrial groups opposed the passage of the Wagner bill. Speaking for the U.S. Steel Corporation, Arthur H. Young opposed the bill's provisions outlawing company unions and assured the Senators that a company union was a "supplement to the Golden Rule." By 1934 Tom Girdler had moved from Jones & Laughlin to become president of the Republic Steel Corporation. He assured the committee that there had never been any labor trouble at the Jones & Laughlin Aliquippa plant because of the "direct personal contact between our management and our men." The Wagner bill, Girdler maintained, would encourage the unionization of employees and would interfere with this beneficial, direct personal relationship between employers and employees.

The situation in the steel industry in 1934 appeared to belie the picture of peaceful employer-employee relations that was given to the Senate committee by Girdler. An industry-wide strike was threatened in steel by the Amalgamated Association of Iron, Steel and Tin Workers on the issue of union recognition. The industry uniformly rejected this demand for union recognition, and a group of "progressive" rank and file union members threatened "bloody war" unless the industry bargained with the union. The union members were called to Washington to confer with NLB and NRA officials in an attempt to settle the issue, but to no avail. The unionists denounced the NRA as the "National Run Around," and in a letter to President Roosevelt declared that they had "lost faith in your administration, which promised justice and a new deal to the workers of the nation."

Despite massive business opposition, the Wagner bill's prospects in Congress brightened when it was reported favorably by the Senate committee. Roosevelt, however, faced with the threatened strike in steel, proposed that Congress pass a resolution creating a National Labor Relations Board that would have the responsibility of enforcing Section 7 (a), holding representation elections, and hearing cases involving employer discrimination against union members. As a political leader Roosevelt was not particularly interested in the problems of organized labor or sympathetic to efforts to protect the right of labor to organize and bargain collectively. He was also generally suspicious of the leadership of organized labor. The result of his feelings meant that the special problems of union labor ranked rather low in the priorities of his administration.

Secretary of Labor Frances Perkins, a former social worker, was more interested in programs of general social reform than the issue of the right to organize. In a program she outlined to Roosevelt at the outset of the administration, Secretary Perkins listed unemployment compensation, public works, minimum wages, maximum hours, federal employment agencies, and the abolition of child labor as high priority items, but governmental protection of the right to organize was not among the items in her program. Organized labor's access to the administration was therefore quite limited as far as its own special problems were concerned. Some members of Congress, such as Robert Wagner, were far more responsive to union problems than the administration. It is in light of these factors that Roosevelt's undercutting of the Wagner bill during 1934 may be understood.

Despite the generally favorable signs that the Wagner bill

would pass, the effect of Roosevelt's proposal was to block the passage of the Wagner bill in 1934. The New Dealers in Congress bowed to the administration's wishes and passed Public Resolution No. 44 creating the NLRB, but not without considerable grumbling. In the Senate, Senator La Follette of Wisconsin offered the Wagner bill as a substitute for Resolution No. 44, but Wagner, loyally supporting the administration, was constrained to ask La Follette to withdraw his proposal in what Wagner confessed was "one of the most embarrassing moments of my whole political life." To Senator Cutting of New Mexico, Public Resolution No. 44 meant that the New Deal was being "strangled in the house of its friends."

Although the NLRB created by Public Resolution No. 44 was composed entirely of public members and possessed a permanent staff, its record in enforcing Section 7 (a) of the NIRA was similar to the old NLB. The protection of the right of workers to organize continued to be ineffective. Dean Lloyd K. Garrison of the University of Wisconsin Law School declared early in 1935, after a brief tenure as chairman of the NLRB, that Section 7 (a) could never "be enforced with even-handed justice, under the existing administrative machinery. . . . The powers of the Board, which is the chief governmental agency dealing with 7-a cases, are quite inadequate for the proper discharge of its responsibilities." The NLRB's effectiveness was further diminished in late 1934 when Roosevelt ordered the Board to cease assuming jurisdiction over cases involving industries whose NIRA codes provided for industry labor boards. These special industry labor boards, such as the NSLRB, were more often than not virtually paralyzed due to the inability of the employer and labor representatives, of which they were in part composed, to agree on the fundamental issues of majority rule and union recognition.

During the NIRA period, it was obvious that the administration was seeking economic recovery as its primary goal, to the exclusion of effective enforcement of Section 7 (a) if necessary. Economic recovery under the NIRA from 1933 to 1935 was based upon a recognition of the dominance of employer groups. In every major confrontation in this period between the administration and employer groups on the issue of the right to organize, the employer groups won, with the administration usually making concessions for the sake of unity behind the recovery effort. Although union membership increased by an estimated one million during this period, many industries, like the steel industry, responded to the threat of unionization posed by Section 7 (a) by establishing company unions. Membership in company unions increased at a greater rate during the NIRA period than membership in bona fide unions.

The *Schechter* Case

Whatever minimal restraints the NIRA imposed upon employer interference with the right of labor to organize was destroyed on May 27, 1935 when the Supreme Court unanimously held that the act was unconstitutional. The policy of the Justice Department in delaying as long as possible a Supreme Court test of the validity of the NIRA, rather than seeking out the best possible case in which the act could have been defended, resulted in a test of the act in perhaps the worst possible case from the government's point of view. The government was ultimately constrained to defend the NIRA, not as applied to the steel, automobile, or some other basic and major industry, but as applied to the live poultry industry in New York City.

Under the provisions of the NIRA Live Poultry Code various unfair and harmful practices were outlawed in the industry—such as selling tubercular chickens. Additionally, the code prescribed minimum wage and maximum hour standards governing the employment of workers in the industry. The

Schechter Poultry Corporation slaughtered poultry and resold it to local retail dealers and butchers. The corporation was charged by the government with violating several provisions of the Live Poultry Code including selling sick chickens and violating the minimum wage and maximum hour provisions of the code. The Schechter Corporation was prosecuted in the District Court for the Eastern District of New York, where the government won a favorable judgment. The Schechter Corporation then appealed to the U.S. Court of Appeals for the Second Circuit, which upheld the conviction for violating the nonlabor provisions of the code. The Court of Appeals ruled, however, that the conviction for violation of the labor provisions of the code was invalid because such regulations were beyond the power of Congress to enact. The Schechter Corporation then appealed the Court of Appeals' affirmation of its conviction for violating the nonlabor provisions of the code to the Supreme Court, and as a result the government was forced into a defense of the constitutional validity of the NIRA in a very weak case.

The strongest argument the government made in support of the validity of the NIRA was based on the *Swift* (1905), *Stafford* (1922), and *Olsen* (1923) stream of commerce cases. The government pointed out that 96 percent of the poultry sold in New York City came from out of state, and that the activities of the Schechter Corporation were thus activities or practices that substantially affected a constantly recurring stream of interstate commerce. In Schechter Poultry Corporation v. United States, 295 U.S. 495 (1935), the Supreme Court nonetheless invalidated the NIRA on the grounds that the act involved an unconstitutional delegation of legislative power to the President and that its provisions exceeded congressional power under the Commerce Clause. Chief Justice Hughes, after having examined the NIRA's provisions relating to the delegation of legislative power to the President, held that in view of the few restrictions imposed by the act upon his exercise of the power delegated to him, "the discretion of the President in approving and prescribing codes, and thus enacting laws for the government of trade and industry throughout the country, is virtually unfettered. We think that the code-making authority thus conferred is an unconstitutional delegation of legislative power."

The Court then turned to an examination of the NIRA's validity under the Commerce Clause and found it constitutionally defective on that ground also. The activities of the Schechter Poultry Corporation, the Court held, were entirely intrastate in nature. When the poultry handled by the Schechter Corporation arrived in New York City by rail or otherwise, Hughes said, the "interstate transactions in relation to that poultry then ended." The Schechter Corporation then "held the poultry at their slaughterhouse markets for slaughter and local sale to retail dealers and butchers, who in turn sold directly to consumers. Neither the slaughtering nor sales by defendants were transactions in interstate commerce." The Court specifically rejected the stream of commerce argument advanced by the government to support the NIRA's validity under the Commerce Clause:

> The mere fact that there may be a constant flow of commodities into a State does not mean that the flow continues after the property has arrived and has become commingled with the mass of property within the State and is there held solely for local disposition and use. So far as the poultry herein questioned is concerned, the flow in interstate commerce had ceased. The poultry had come to a permanent rest within the State. . . . Hence decisions which deal with a stream of interstate commerce—where goods come to rest within a State temporarily and are later to go forward in interstate commerce—and with the regulations of transportation involved in that practical continuity of movement, are not applicable here.

The Court conceded that Congress under the Commerce Clause could reach even essentially local or intrastate activities which had "direct" effects upon interstate commerce. In the railroad cases, the Court said, it had sustained congressional regulation of concededly intrastate matters because such matters affected interstate commerce directly. In determining the degree to which Congress could reach intrastate or local activities having an effect upon commerce, the Court said, "there is a necessary and well-established distinction between direct and indirect effects. The precise line can be drawn only as individual cases arise, but the distinction is clear in principle." When intrastate transactions only affected interstate commerce indirectly, the Court said:

> . . . such transactions remain within the domain of State power. If the commerce clause were construed to reach all enterprises and transactions which could be said to have an indirect effect upon interstate commerce, the Federal authority would embrace practically all the activities of the people and the authority of the State over its domestic concerns would exist only by sufferance of the Federal Government.

In the Court's view, therefore, the distinction between direct and indirect effects had to be "recognized as a fundamental one, essential to the maintenance of our constitutional system. Otherwise, as we have said, there would be virtually no limit to the Federal power, and for all practical purposes we should have a completely centralized government." The Court held that since the activities of the Schechter Poultry Corporation affected interstate commerce only indirectly, the NIRA as applied to it was unconstitutional.

The Court's emphasis upon the direct-indirect effects formula in the *Schechter* case (1935) was of course reminiscent of the Sugar Trust case (1895) and similar cases in which it had attempted to separate and confine federal and state power in rigid constitutional compartments. This approach to the commerce power was understandably depressing to New Dealers. President Roosevelt was apparently surprised that the liberals on the Court, Cardozo, Brandeis, and Stone, had joined in the unanimous invalidation of the NIRA.

Informed of the Court's decision in the *Schechter* case, Roosevelt asked, "Well where was Ben Cardozo? How did he stand? And what about old Isaiah [Brandeis]?" Four days after the decision, the President attacked the Court's action for over an hour during his press conference. The Court's opinion in the *Schechter* case, he declared, contained a "horse-and-buggy definition of interstate commerce."

The *Alton Railroad* Case

A further indication in 1935 that the Court would strictly construe congressional power under the Commerce Clause was manifested in its decision in Railroad Retirement Board v. Alton Railroad Company, 295 U.S. 330 (1935). In the *Alton* case, the Court invalidated by a five to four vote the Railroad Retirement Act of 1933 that provided for old age pensions for employees of interstate carriers. Despite the long line of railroad cases that supported a very broad congressional power over interstate railroads, Justice Roberts joined Justices Sutherland, Butler, Van Devanter, and McReynolds in holding the Retirement Act invalid under the Commerce Clause.* The government had defended the act as one which promoted contentment and assurance on the part of railroad workers, thus contributing to the efficiency of interstate rail operations. Justice Roberts, however, writing for the majority, held that:

> . . . a pension plan thus imposed is in no proper sense a regulation of the activity of interstate transportation. It is an attempt for social ends to impose by sheer fiat non-contractual incidents upon the relation of employer and employee, not as a rule or regulation of commerce and transportation between the States, but as a means of assuring a particular class of employees against old age dependency. This is neither a necessary nor an appropriate

---

* The Retirement Act was also invalidated by the majority on the grounds that it deprived the carriers of their property without due process of law in violation of the Fifth Amendment.

rule or regulation affecting the due fulfilment of the railroads' duty to serve the public in interstate transportation.

Taken together, the *Schechter* (1935) and *Alton* (1935) cases thus cast a pall over the viability of both the stream of commerce and the railroad cases as precedents upon which to base a defense of broad enactments under the Commerce Clause. Instead of following such precedents, the Court had chosen the more restrictive line of precedents under the Commerce Clause—precedents which embodied the Sugar Trust case (1895) conception of interstate commerce.

The invalidation of the NIRA in the *Schechter* case (1935) had the further effect of removing the minimal restraint upon employers which the labor board system and Section 7 (a) had imposed. In Aliquippa the intervention of the NSLRB and Governor Pinchot during 1934 had resulted in a greater degree of freedom for union organizers and union members than had ever existed in "Little Siberia." After the invalidation of the NIRA in the *Schechter* case, however, Jones & Laughlin resumed pressure tactics against the unionization of its employees. To some observers the intimidation and coercion of its employees became even greater after the *Schechter* case than it had been before the coming of the New Deal.

Senator Wagner, however, had refused to cease his efforts to obtain permanent legislation guaranteeing the right of labor to organize and bargain collectively and prohibiting employer interference with that right through effective enforcement machinery, despite the temporary defeat he had suffered when the administration had sponsored the temporary Public Resolution No. 44 approach to the problem. Indeed, Wagner had succeeded in winning Senate approval of his labor relations bill by a vote of 63 to 12 eleven days before the Court's decision in the *Schechter* case (1935). And this time, faced with the likelihood that the Wagner bill would pass the House with a large majority, President Roosevelt belatedly endorsed the bill three days before the *Schechter* decision. The passage of the National Labor Relations Act (Wagner Act) by the Congress in June 1935 began the epic constitutional battle of the New Deal period. Its climax in 1937 was a major turning point not only for the New Deal but for the whole course of American constitutional development.

✦ 3 ✦

THE ORDEAL OF THE NLRB

The National Labor Relations Act was the object of massive campaigns of opposition in both the legislature and judiciary. Senator Wagner had been defeated in his attempt to win congressional approval of the NLRA in 1934 by the administration's support for the temporary expedient of Public Resolution No. 44. In 1935 Wagner renewed his campaign for his labor relations bill and won congressional approval of it. The prestige of the business community had been dealt a formidable blow by the depression and the torrent of New Deal legislation had left many businessmen in a state of shock. "We feel there should be a cessation of more of the so-called reform legislation," one businessman told Congress in 1934. "We have got mental indigestion, trying to keep up." The business community exhibited not only shock as the New Deal years wore on, but also increasingly demonstrated both fear and hatred as what were considered the cherished American values of self-reliance and individualism were trampled under foot by the New Deal and as the spectre of socialism began to haunt the business community.

THE REVOLT OF THE CONSERVATIVES

The principal strategy utilized by business groups during the New Deal period was to confront each New Deal measure that adversely affected business with the Constitution. The Constitution, it was argued, embodied guarantees of individual liberty and limitations upon governmental power that were being ignored by the federal government in a massive assault upon traditional American values and principles of government. Unlike the period following the Civil War, business interests during the New Deal period were not creative or innovative forces seeking change in constitutional interpretation but rather they were seeking the application by the courts of such existing constitutional doctrines as liberty of contract, dual federalism, and the direct-indirect effects formula. Because these doctrines were to a great extent the prevailing constitutional interpretations being accepted by the courts, by appealing to the "immutable" and "sacred" principles of the Constitution during the 1930s, business groups could utilize the symbolic value of the Constitution as a political weapon in their struggle against the New Deal. The utilization of the Constitution as a political symbol is characteristic of American politics. Throughout our history this practice has been used by individuals and groups who find themselves disadvantaged in the electoral process or the victims of governmental policies adversely affecting their interests.

This utilization of the Constitution as a symbol in politics by business interests was, however, not altogether unconscious. During 1934 the former chairman of the Democratic National Committee, John J. Raskob, began a correspondence with business leaders on the subject of the disastrously low prestige of the business community and the dangers this condition involved for business in the political process. Raskob suggested to one business executive closely connected with the DuPont and General Motors organizations that he "take the lead in trying to induce the DuPont and General Motors groups, followed by the other big industries, to definitely organize to protect society from the sufferings which it is bound to endure if we allow communistic elements to lead the people to believe all businessmen are crooks." Out of Raskob's concern and a similar concern by many other business leaders, the American Liberty League was founded in August 1934. The Liberty League was financed from DuPont and General Motors funds and became the most publicized business group in opposition to the New Deal, attracting to its ranks many prominent Democrats who had become disillusioned with the New Deal and the direction in which the Democratic Party under Franklin Roosevelt was moving. These people included Al Smith and John W. Davis, the Democratic presidential candidates in 1928 and 1924 respectively, and John J. Raskob, the former chairman of the Democratic National Committee.

In its attacks on the New Deal, the Liberty League utilized the symbolic value of the Constitution to its fullest. During the formative stages of the league a confidential memorandum was circulated among the league's prospective supporters suggesting that "however efficient such an organization may be, it will have great difficulty in accomplishing its work unless it has a moral or emotional purpose, and thereby creates a moral or emotional issue." Such an issue, the author of the memorandum argued, was the issue of the Constitution itself, since there were not many issues which could:

> . . . command more support or evoke more enthusiasm among our people than the simple issue of the "Constitution." . . . The public interest concerning it is dense and inexperienced, but, nevertheless, there is a mighty, though vague, affection for it. The people, I believe, need merely to be led and instructed, and this affection will become almost worship and can be converted into an

irresistible movement. . . . I think our first appeal should be to
the effect that the Constitution is perfect; we do not seek to
change it, or to add or to subtract from it; we seek to rescue it
from those who misunderstand it, misuse it and mistreat it. . . .
And we should remember that he who takes the "Constitution"
for his battle-cry, has as his allies the Fathers of old. It will be of
inestimable aid to quote Washington, Franklin, Hamilton, Adams,
Jefferson, Madison, Monroe and other mighty men of the past,
and to recall the Supreme Court's stirring opinions handed down
by Marshall and his fellow justices.*

This Liberty League memorandum stated in capsule form
the essential strategy not only of the league but of most other
business groups against the New Deal.   In the phrases of
league spokesmen, the New Deal was thus "gnawing at the vi-
tals of the Constitution" and could lead to the "death of democratic institutions."   "The issue is not whether the Constitution shall be amended, but whether it shall be destroyed."
Along with defense of the Constitution against the New Deal,
the Liberty League also defended the Supreme Court as an
institution that had "always thrown the powerful circle of
the Constitution as a defense around the humblest as well as
the greatest of American citizens . . . [and it was] the one last
thin line that had stood between the American people and
the destruction of the form of government in which they
believe."

THE ENACTMENT OF THE NLRA

Against no other New Deal measure were these polemics of
constitutionalism directed more earnestly and vehemently
than against the National Labor Relations Act.   The Roosevelt administration had headed off the NLRA in 1934 with the
expedient of temporary labor boards under Public Resolution

---

* The memorandum is quoted in George Wolfskill, *The Revolt of the
Conservatives* (Boston: Houghton Mifflin, 1962), pp. 111–112. Captain
William H. Slayton wrote the memorandum.

No. 44, but Senator Wagner returned to the fight in 1935 and reintroduced the labor relations bill in the Senate. The National Association of Manufacturers coordinated the battle that was waged by business groups against the bill in 1935. As the Senate Committee on Education and Labor scheduled hearings on the bill the NAM contacted business leaders urging their appearance as witnesses against the bill. The business community, the NAM said, had to "meet the onslaught of union fostered attacks. . . . This is the most important cooperation the NAM ever asked of you." In addition to recruiting business witnesses to appear in the Senate hearings in opposition to the labor relations bill, a letter writing campaign directed at Congress was also organized by the business community. This campaign, however, reached its peak too soon and was faltering by the time the Wagner bill was being voted on in Congress. The business community's attack on the bill in Congress also suffered from the fact that almost all of the arguments against it had been rehearsed in the 1934 Senate hearing on the bill, and by 1935 hardly anything new could be said in opposition to the bill that had not already been said many times before.

James A. Emery, general counsel for the NAM, opened the business attack on the bill in the Senate hearings on March 21. "The first day of spring, Mr. Chairman," Emery said at the outset, "is marked by consideration of an exotic in legislation, which we trust will find little favor in your cultivated consideration." Emery proceeded to attack the bill on the same constitutional grounds that would be repeated over and over for the following two years. Invoking the doctrine of dual federalism, Emery charged that the act violated the Tenth Amendment of the Constitution by invading the reserved powers of the states, since under the bill's terms manufacturing and production enterprises would be subject to its provisions. Congress, Emery argued, was simply foreclosed by the Constitution from regulating production enterprises under the Commerce Clause. In addition he said that the bill violated the liberty of contract guaranteed by the Fifth Amendment's Due Process Clause by interfering with the right of employers to hire whom they chose and the right of employees to bargain individually with their employers.

Following Emery's presentation a long list of representatives of business and industrial groups appeared in opposition to the bill. One of the most effectively organized industry groups was the steel industry, which began its appearance before the Senate committee on March 26. Not only did steel executives testify against the bill, but employees in the steel industry were recruited to testify in favor of the company unions in the steel industry and to indicate that the majority of the steel workers favored the company unions to bona fide labor unions. The employee representative of the Jones & Laughlin Employees' Representation Plan at Aliquippa, for example, testified that a majority of the workers there preferred the company union and that the local of the Amalgamated Association of Iron, Steel and Tin Workers at Aliquippa was then defunct. According to this Jones & Laughlin employee, an Amalgamated organizer had been sent to Aliquippa:

> . . . but he was withdrawn when the Pittsburgh papers published a story showing that he had been guilty of a criminal assault on his ten-year-old stepdaughter. . . . Two weeks ago, one of their members was found guilty of felonious assault and battery in the Beaver Court, after he had stabbed one of our employees because he refused to join the Amalgamated. It is not surprising that our workmen have shown their preference to our plan.

Such testimony was regarded as sufficiently damaging to the union cause that the AFL transported members of the Aliquippa local of the Amalgamated to testify before the Senate committee a few days later. The union spokesmen presented an opposite view to the one that the Jones & Laughlin company union representative presented. They also gave the committee a black picture of conditions in Aliquippa. Contrary

to the previous testimony the union spokesmen asserted that
the union had organized a majority of the Jones & Laughlin
employees at Aliquippa but that the company was firing men
"just lately for the least little thing, without any reason what-
soever. . . . Our men are scared," the union witnesses said,
"and they have—the company—spies all over the street following us."

The wholesale attack by business on the bill continued,
however, and on April 2 James A. Emery again appeared to
round out the opposition of business to the bill.   Emery cited
to the Senate committee twenty cases that had been decided by
the lower federal courts during the NIRA period, all of which
had held that Congress could not regulate production or manufacturing industries under the Commerce Clause. He again
declared that the labor relations bill violated liberty of contract—the right, Emery said, "of a man to make a contract to
enter into engagements for the sale of his labor or for the sale
of his goods or for the sale of his talent or for the sale of his
services in any way he pleases. . . ." "Freedom of contract,"
Emery declared, "is the rule and restraint the exception."

While the attack by business and industrial groups on the
Wagner bill was conducted on a massive scale it appears to
have had little impact upon the overwhelmingly pro-New
Deal Senate.   More bothersome to Senator Wagner was the
ambivalent if not hostile attitude of the Roosevelt administration to the labor relations bill.   Wagner had sought the President's endorsement of his bill in 1935, but he was successful in
obtaining only a promise from Roosevelt that the administration would not oppose it, a promise that was not entirely kept.
General Hugh Johnson and Donald Richberg, officials high in
the National Recovery Administration, utilized every opportunity to scuttle the bill short of public opposition.   Secretary
of Labor Perkins appeared lukewarm in her support, although
she lobbied effectively for the lodging of the National Labor
Relations Board in the Department of Labor. When Senate

consideration of the bill was imminent Roosevelt called Senator Wagner to the White House, where in Roosevelt's presence Senate Democratic Leader Joe Robinson and Senate stalwart Pat Harrison sought unsuccessfully to convince Wagner to drop the bill. It is one of the great ironies of the history of the New Deal that the National Labor Relations Act is usually regarded as epitomizing the New Deal and yet the Roosevelt administration had nothing to do with its drafting and little to do with its passage by Congress.

In addition to business opposition and the indifference if not hostility of the administration, the Wagner bill was also overwhelmingly opposed by the press including such leading columnists as Walter Lippmann. "If the bill were passed," Lippmann said, "it could not be made to work. . . . It is preposterous to put such a burden on mortal man. . . . The bill should, I believe, be scrapped." The liberal American Civil Liberties Union also initially opposed the Wagner bill. Identifying governmental action as posing the traditional threat to civil liberties, the ACLU at first opposed the bill, but because of internal opposition within the Union, later adopted a neutral position. The Communist Party, however, strongly opposed the Wagner bill as an attempt by the ruling class to dupe the American worker.

The Senate nevertheless passed the Wagner bill on May 16 by an overwhelming vote of sixty-three to twelve. It was only at this point that the President began to move away from his previously ambivalent position on the bill. Nine days after the passage of the bill in the Senate Roosevelt called Wagner, Sidney Hillman of the Amalgamated Clothing Workers, and John L. Lewis of the United Mine Workers to the White House for a conference with administration officials, and following the conference the President endorsed the bill. The legislative assistant to Wagner who aided in drafting the bill, Leon Keyserling, has concluded that "Franklin D. Roosevelt . . . gave the legislation his tepid public blessing only after it became clear to him that the bill would be forced to a decision by its sponsor and that it would pass both houses of Congress overwhelmingly whether he endorsed it or not."

The constitutional arguments against the bill which had been used in the Senate hearings were repeated in the debate on the bill in the House of Representatives. "We have," one of the bill's opponents declared, "the remarkable situation of the legislative and executive branches deliberately and willfully engaged in enacting legislation to vest powers in the administrative branch which powers they know the Constitution says are not within the jurisdiction of the Federal Government." And Representative Cox of Georgia argued that the "purpose of the measure, as all honest minds must confess, is to circumvent the effect of the recent ruling of the Supreme Court in the *Schechter case.*" "Is there a good lawyer in this House," another opponent asked, "who for one moment believes that such a law would be upheld by the Supreme Court? Certainly it will not stand. Passing this bill is a futile thing. It is a mere gesture." Representative Truax of Ohio replied to the constitutional arguments that the opponents of the bill raised by castigating the Supreme Court for elevating property rights over human rights in its decisions. "What are you going to do with this sacred old Constitution?" Truax asked the bill's opponents. "You cannot eat it, you cannot wear it, and you cannot sleep in it."

The House passed the bill with minor amendments by a voice vote, and it was ultimately referred to a conference committee to iron out the differences between the Senate and House versions. The conference committee report was adopted by both houses on June 17, ending the congressional battle. The President signed the National Labor Relations Act into law on July 5, reading a statement that defended the act's constitutionality. The NLRA, Roosevelt said:

> . . . does not cover all industry and labor, but is applicable only when violation of the legal right of independent self-organization

would burden or obstruct interstate commerce. Accepted by management, labor, and the public with a sense of sober responsibility and of willing cooperation, however, it should serve as an important step toward the achievement of justice and peaceful relations in industry.

Wagner, Keyserling, and the others responsible for drafting the NLRA had been acutely aware all along that the legislative battle over the act would only be a prelude to a great constitutional battle in the courts on the validity of the act. The Supreme Court's decision in the *Schechter* case on May 27, 1935 and its emphasis on the direct-indirect effects formula in that case only served to heighten the awareness of the act's sponsors to its vulnerability on constitutional grounds. As a result of the *Schechter* case Wagner had obtained recommittal of the act to the House Labor Committee so that the constitutional basis of the act could be tightened up. The NLRA thus ultimately contained a "Finding and Policy" by Congress that held that the denial of the right of workers to organize and bargain collectively by employers led:

> . . . to strikes and other forms of industrial strife or unrest, which have the intent or necessary effect of burdening or obstructing . . . commerce by (a) impairing the efficiency, safety, or operation of the instrumentalities of commerce; (b) occurring in the current of commerce; (c) materially affecting, restraining, or controlling the flow of raw materials or manufactured or processed goods from or into the channels of commerce; or (d) causing dimunition of employment and wages in such volume as substantially to impair or disrupt the market for goods flowing from or into the channels of commerce.

The "Finding and Policy" also stated that protection of the right of workers to organize and bargain collectively "safeguards commerce from injury, impairment, or interruption, and promotes the flow of commerce by removing certain recognized sources of industrial strife and unrest. . . ."

The "Finding and Policy" in the NLRA was thus based upon the language used by the Supreme Court itself in numerous cases in which it had defined the scope of congressional power to regulate interstate commerce. It also contained a congressional finding that the unequal bargaining position of workers, which was due to their lack of "full freedom of association or actual liberty of contract," had the effect of depressing wages and aggravating economic depressions. The labor department lawyers who had participated in drafting the "Finding and Policy" objected to the inclusion of this language because they felt it detracted from the Commerce Clause basis of the act, but Senator Wagner insisted that the language be left in. Wagner continued to believe that the real purpose of his labor relations act was to make the American worker a "free man," and he never entirely accepted the Commerce Clause rationale of the act which emphasized the reduction of obstructions and burdens on commerce caused by strikes as the chief purpose of the act.

Wagner nevertheless defended the Commerce Clause basis of the act against arguments that the Court's *Schechter* decision (1935) doomed the NLRA. He said that:

> The Court has made it clear in a long series of decisions, that the issue of whether a practice "directly" affects interstate commerce, and thus is subject to federal regulation, depends more upon the nature of the practice than upon the area of activity of the business in which the practice occurs. It is clear that the *Schechter* decision limits federal supervision of wages and hours in situations where federal efforts to maintain industrial peace, and thus prevent interference with the physical flow of goods, would be sustained.

The NLRA thus applied to all businesses in which a labor dispute would interrupt, burden, or obstruct interstate commerce or affect such commerce.

The act contained a list of "unfair labor practices" that prohibited employers from interfering with the exercise of their employees' right to organize, from dominating or financing a company union, and from discharging employees or otherwise discriminating against employees in regard to terms and conditions of employment for the purpose of discouraging union membership. Refusal of an employer to bargain collectively with his employees was also an unfair labor practice.

The NLRA created a three-man National Labor Relations Board to be appointed by the President. The Board was authorized to hold elections among employees within particular bargaining units to determine whether a majority of the employees desired union representation. If a majority of the employees voted in favor of a union then the union would be certified by the NLRB as the exclusive bargaining agent for all of the employees in the bargaining unit. The Board was also empowered to investigate charges by unions or employees that employers were committing unfair labor practices. If the charges were determined by the Board to have merit, a hearing would be held during which both the union or workers and the employer could present evidence to support their positions. If the Board found after a hearing that an employer had committed an unfair labor practice, it could order the employer to cease and desist from the practice; if workers had been fired by an employer for union membership, a typical NLRB order would be to require the employer to rehire the workers and compensate them for the wages lost because of their having been fired. To enforce its orders, however, the Board was required to seek an enforcement order from the appropriate U.S. court of appeals; employers who were subject to Board orders could also seek review of the orders in the courts of appeals.*

THE ASSAULT ON THE NLRB

No other governmental agency in our history has ever been faced with as many severe problems in merely surviving as

* At this time the U.S. courts of appeals were referred to as the "circuit courts of appeals." I shall use the modern designation herein.

those faced by the NLRB between 1935 and 1937. Roosevelt did not appoint the three members of the Board until late August 1935. As chairman of the Board the President appointed J. Warren Madden, a professor of law at the University of Pittsburgh. The other members of the NLRB were John M. Carmody, a member of the National Mediation Board, and Edwin S. Smith, a former member of the old Public Resolution No. 44 NLRB. Fortunately for the Board much of the permanent staff of the old NLRB remained intact, thus allowing the new Board to avoid the problem of completely restaffing. The Washington office of the NLRB in 1935 consisted of fifty-three employees and a total of sixty-three NLRB employees were scattered over the country in twenty-one field offices.

The staff that the NLRB inherited was rather dismayed with Madden's selection as chairman since he had not previously been identified with the cause of labor. The staff consisted mostly of labor relations specialists who were also skeptical of the Board's emphasis upon the necessity of defending the NLRA in cases prepared with the greatest legal competence possible. Despite the misgivings of the staff, however, the Board decided that in view of the grave constitutional doubts as to the NLRA's validity, each NLRB regional office should be staffed with a regional attorney who would work with the regional director but would be under the direct supervision of the Board's General Counsel in Washington. The general counsel of the old NLRB was asked to remain with the new Board but he preferred to return to private life. He recommended Charles Fahy who had been the chairman of the Petroleum Labor Board. Fahy accepted the position of General Counsel, and directed the strategy by which the NLRA would be defended in the courts with great skill. He would later serve as U.S. Solicitor General and as a judge on the Court of Appeals for the District of Columbia.

Nine days after the President appointed the members of the NLRB the Liberty League issued a public report on the constitutionality of the NLRA. Fifty-eight leading corporation attorneys signed the report which had been written by eight Liberty League attorneys under the chairmanship of Earl F. Reed, the counsel for the Weirton Steel Company. Among those signing the report were James M. Beck and John W. Davis, both former U.S. Solicitors General. Davis had also been the Democratic presidential candidate in 1924. The Liberty League report stated that the times "and our economy may have changed, but we have not changed our Constitution nor even deemed it advisable so to do. It is our task to expound our constitutional law as it is, apart from its economical or social consequences. . . ." *

The report emphasized at the outset that the direct-indirect effects formula utilized by the Supreme Court in the *Schechter* case (1935) was a fundamental command of the Constitution, and while local activities might affect interstate commerce indirectly, this "is no excuse for attacking the Court for distinguishing between commerce and that which is not commerce, a distinction which the Constitution required it to obey." In interpreting the Constitution, the Liberty League report said, the Court was merely implementing the mandate that the people had imposed upon themselves.

> We have, ourselves, . . . deliberately created limitations on our powers as a people, not merely to restrain our governors, but also to restrain our own temporary beliefs and enthusiasms. Settled opinions of the people, in the long run, will and do make use of the machinery which the Constitution itself provides for its amendment, but in brief periods of temporary frenzy, the Constitution and the Supreme Court justly hold us to the limits that we, ourselves, have established.

The report argued that the NLRA not only attempted to regulate local activities affecting commerce only indirectly, but it also invaded the reserved powers of the states protected by

* National Lawyers' Committee (Library League) , *Report on the Constitutionality of the National Labor Relations Act* (Pittsburgh: Smith Brothers, 1935) .

the Tenth Amendment. The act also could not be sustained under the stream of commerce cases, such as *Stafford* v. *Wallace* (1922) and *Chicago Board of Trade* v. *Olsen* (1923), because the authors of the report considered the stream of commerce cases to be highly isolated applications of the Commerce Clause that were not relevant to the employer-employee relationship at the local level. The NLRA was therefore invalid under the Commerce Clause because even though "relations between employers and employees, whether peaceful or hostile, may have some bearing upon interstate commerce, . . . the bearing is too remote to permit . . . regulation. A succession of speculative possibilities cannot substitute for the direct relation the cases discussed require."

The Liberty League report also concluded that the NLRA was invalid under the Fifth Amendment's Due Process Clause because it interfered unreasonably with liberty of contract between employers and employees. The act's prohibition of unfair labor practices, the league lawyers argued, was an attempt to "force a novel economic policy" into the employer-employee relationship. The act's provision that a majority of employees in a particular bargaining unit could determine the exclusive bargaining agent for all of the employees in such a unit, the report said, denied liberty of contract to the individual employee by prohibiting him from bargaining individually for terms and conditions of work with his employer. The act's provisions prohibiting employers from discharging or otherwise discriminating against employees because of their union membership, it was also argued, interfered with the liberty of contract of employers which under the doctrine of the *Adair* (1908) and *Coppage* (1915) cases protected the employer's right to hire whom he chose. The report also rejected the contention that the *Texas & New Orleans Railroad* case, sustaining the validity of the Railway Labor Act in 1930, had reversed the *Adair* and *Coppage* cases.

The NLRA, the Liberty League report concluded, was

wholly unconstitutional on both the Commerce Clause and due process grounds. The report said:

> We have examined the Act with a view to expressing our opinion as to its constitutionality and whether or not it represents a departure from our established system of government. . . . Considering the Act in the light of our history, the established form of government, and the decisions of our highest Court, we have no hesitancy in concluding that it is unconstitutional and that it constitutes a complete departure from our constitutional and traditional theories of government.

The Liberty League report holding the NLRA unconstitutional was only one of several such denunciations of the act by business groups. Immediately after the passage of the NLRA, for example, the NAM distributed twelve thousand copies of a legal opinion to its membership advising them of the constitutional issues raised by the act. As far as the Commerce Clause basis of the act was concerned, the NAM opinion informed industrialists that the act:

> . . . does not apply to employment relations between a manufacturer and his employees engaged in ordinary manufacturing operations. The Act is based upon the power of Congress to regulate interstate and foreign commerce. Manufacturing is not commerce at all. Commerce does not begin until manufacturing has ended. The employment relations at issue arise *in production* and not intercourse. This rule has been uniformly adhered to by the Supreme Court of the United States.

The NAM opinion concluded that the NLRA was wholly invalid because of its interference with liberty of contract. "By denying to an individual employee his fundamental right to bargain or contract with his employer," the NAM said, "without associating with a group, we believe the majority rule principle is invalid for reasons expressed by the Supreme Court of the United States in *Adair* v. *U.S.* . . . and *Coppage* v. *Kansas*. . . ." The NAM advised manufacturers that if the NLRB should move against them, they should be careful to make a full response to any of the Board's charges and to object to the Board's jurisdiction over them on constitutional grounds. Manufacturers should also consider, the NAM advised, making an appearance through counsel at any NLRB hearings in order to ensure that the record in the proceeding reflected the manufacturer's side of the case. "It must be remembered," the NAM said, "that on appeal the courts will review the record before the Board, and in some cases the nature of the record may determine the character of the court's decision."

The NAM formed in 1935 the National Industrial Information Committee because of its concern over the low prestige of the business community. The committee was chaired by Ernest T. Weir of the Weirton Steel Company and had the purpose of counteracting the "hazard facing industrialists" because of "the newly realized power of the masses." Unless the "masses" were directed toward sound thinking, the committee said, "we are definitely headed for adversity." The committee thus conducted an "information" program which concentrated on popularizing classical economics, attacking the expansion of governmental power during the New Deal, and defending conservative constitutional principles.

While the Liberty League and the NAM were the most prominent leaders of the constitutional attack by business upon the NLRA, other more specialized business groups followed their lead. The American Newspaper Publishers Association, for example, advised newspaper publishers through its legal counsel that the NLRA was "unconstitutional beyond question or doubt." And in a legal opinion issued by the ANPA in 1936, publishers were advised that they:

> . . . should flatly refuse to have anything to do with the National Labor Relations Board, other than to notify it it is without power under the Constitution to interfere with their business. . . . There is, in so far as the business of the press is affected by its terms, the question as to whether Congress has the power to vest an agency of the government with authority to dictate to publish-

ers whom they shall or shall not employ. If the law is valid, that authority has been conferred on a Board, and without limitation. Such a power is now being exercised by the Hitler government in Germany.

No order of the NLRB directed at a publisher would be upheld by the courts, publishers were advised, and they therefore should "tell any National Labor Relations Board representative coming into contact with them that the Board is without jurisdiction and to refuse to deal with such representative."

Earl F. Reed stated that when "a lawyer tells a client that a law is unconstitutional it is then a nullity and he need no longer obey that law." New Dealers attacked such statements and reports as attempts to encourage disobedience of the law and to influence the courts in cases testing the act's validity. The NLRB thus answered the Liberty League report by accusing the corporation lawyers responsible of a "deliberate and concerted effort . . . to undermine public confidence in the [NLRA], to discourage compliance with it, to assist attorneys generally in attacks on the statute, and perhaps to influence the courts."

The Battle Against Injunctions

The public constitutional attacks upon the validity of the NLRA by business groups had the effect of furnishing any attorney defending a client in NLRB proceedings with canned briefs raising every substantial constitutional objection to the act. Between 1935 and 1937 the NLRB was put through an ordeal by litigation involving almost one hundred suits for injunctions against its proceeding against employers. The public denunciation of the NLRA by business groups undoubtedly encouraged such suits. Because of this injunctive attack, the NLRB's first and most serious problem was to escape complete paralyzation by injunction. The first injunction suit against the Board was filed in November 1935, and as the Board said later, the:

> . . . process was like a rolling snowball. The allegations in a pleading filed by an employer in Georgia, for example, would show up in precisely the same wording in a pleading filed in Seattle. There came a very rapid and widespread exchange of pleadings all over the country until all had exhausted their ingenuity in conjuring up the many and gross injuries which it was alleged a hearing before the Board would entail.

Attorneys for employers were able to win some of the injunction suits in federal district courts that were generally hostile to the New Deal. A federal district judge in Missouri, for example, enjoined the NLRB from even holding a hearing on a complaint alleging that an employer was refusing to bargain collectively with his employees. The NLRA as a whole, the judge ruled, was unconstitutional. "The individual employee," he said, "is dealt with by the act as an incompetent. The government must protect him even from himself. He is a ward of the United States to be cared for by his guardian even as if he were a member of an uncivilized tribe of Indians or a recently emancipated slave." The act was not a valid regulation of commerce, the judge continued, since manufacturing was not commerce, and nothing "is more firmly established in constitutional law than that." No one could be found, he said, "who seriously will maintain that interstate commerce *directly* is affected by the manner in which an employer bargains with his employees."

While the problem of paralysis by injunction was the most immediate threat to the NLRB as a result of such suits, a more fundamental threat to the Board was also raised by the injunction litigation. Under the terms of the NLRA, the Board was authorized to hold hearings and to issue orders based upon such hearings, with the courts of appeals having the power to review the Board's actions. This statutory procedure allowed the Board to select its cases carefully and to build the records in its cases with an eye to providing the best possible defense of the act in the courts. The injunction suits, however, threatened to deprive the Board of this advantage and to force it into a position of having to defend the validity of the NLRA before the Supreme Court in an injunction case not of the Board's choosing and lacking a full and complete record upon which the act could have been best defended.

In the injunction suit battle it was therefore crucial that the Board win in order for it to maintain control of the litigation that would ultimately test the validity of the NLRA before the Supreme Court. The uniformity of the pleadings in the injunction suits filed by employers aided the Board in meeting the injunctive attack since Charles Fahy's legal staff could anticipate the allegations such pleadings would contain and prepare appropriate answers in detail as soon as the staff heard of an injunction suit. The Board ultimately won almost three-fourths of the injunction suits in the federal district courts and all but one of the suits in the courts of appeals. The Supreme Court refused in October 1936 to hear a suit in which an employer had been denied an injunction against the NLRB by the lower federal courts. The Board was thus able to maintain the integrity of the NLRA's provisions and to avoid a Supreme Court test of the act's validity in an injunction suit.

THUNDERBOLTS FROM THE COURT

Despite its success in retaining control over the litigation testing the validity of the NLRA, the Board's defense of the act appeared almost hopeless after the Supreme Court's decisions of 1936. In United States v. Butler, 297 U.S. 1 (1936), the Court declared the Agricultural Adjustment Act unconstitutional. The AAA had sought to reduce the overproduction of basic agricultural commodities by offering payments to farmers to restrict the acreage planted in such crops. To finance the payments to farmers the AAA imposed a tax upon the processors of the commodities covered by the act. The Court held in the *Butler* case that the AAA was an attempt by Congress to regulate agricultural production, an activity reserved to the states for regulation by the Tenth Amendment. The *Butler* case thus indicated that the Court would continue to adhere to the doctrine that production was beyond the reach of Congress to regulate.

The most serious blow to the NLRB's hopes of successfully defending the validity of the NLRA came in Carter v. Carter Coal Company, 298 U.S. 238 (1936), in which the Court invalidated the Bituminous Coal Conservation Act. This act provided for minimum prices for soft coal, and for minimum wages, maximum hours, and a guarantee of the right to organize on the part of the workers in the industry. A Bituminous Coal Labor Board was created by the act to enforce the guarantee of the right to organize free from employer interference. In an opinion by Justice Sutherland the Court reiterated the doctrine that manufacturing and mining were local activities distinct from interstate commerce and that Congress could not therefore validly regulate labor relations and conditions of work in the mining industry under the Commerce Clause. Justice Sutherland said that:

> The employment of men, the fixing of their wages, hours of labor and working conditions, the bargaining in respect of these things, whether carried on separately or collectively—each and all constitute intercourse for the purposes of production not of trade. The latter is a thing apart from the relation of employer and employee, which in all producing occupations is purely local in character. . . . [The labor provisions] including those in respect of minimum wages, wage agreements, collective bargaining and the Labor Board and its powers, primarily fall upon production and not commerce; and confirms the further resulting conclusion that production is a purely local activity. It follows that none of these essential antecedents of production constitutes a transaction in or forms any part of interstate commerce. . . . Everything which moves in interstate commerce has had a local origin. Without

local production somewhere, interstate commerce, as now carried on, would practically disappear. Nevertheless, the local character of mining, of manufacturing and of crop growing is a fact, and remains a fact, whatever may be done with the products.

The government in defending the Bituminous Coal Act had leaned heavily upon the stream of commerce concept as enunciated in such cases as the *Swift* (1905), *Stafford* (1922), and *Olsen* (1923) cases. The Court, however, rejected the stream of commerce cases as irrelevant to the *Carter* case (1936). "If the court had held that the raising of cattle, which were involved in the Swift & Co. case," Sutherland said, "including the wages paid to and working conditions of the herders and others employed in the business, could be regulated by Congress, that decision and decisions holding similarly would be in point: for it is that situation, and not the one with which the court actually dealt, which here concerns us." Again the Court emphasized that conditions of labor and the employer-employee relationship were local in nature and affected commerce only indirectly. Sutherland said that:

> The relation of employer and employee, is a local relation. At common law, it is one of the domestic relations. . . . Working conditions are obviously local conditions. The employees are not engaged in or about commerce, but exclusively in producing a commodity. And the controversies and evils, which it is the object of the act to regulate and minimize, are local controversies and evils affecting local work undertaken to accomplish that local result. Such effect as they may have upon commerce, however extensive it may be, is secondary and indirect. An increase in the greatness of the effect adds to its importance. It does not alter its character.

With the Court's decision in the *Carter* case (1936) it thus appeared that the NLRA simply could not validly be applied to any manufacturing or production enterprise. The possibility that the act might be validly applied to clearly interstate businesses was also dimmed by the Court's decision in Morehead v. New York, 298 U.S. 587 (1936). In Adkins v. Children's Hospital, 261 U.S. 525 (1923), the Court had invalidated a minimum wage for women on the grounds that it unreasonably interfered with liberty of contract. Liberty of contract, Justice Sutherland had said in the *Adkins* case, was the rule "and restraint the exception." The act under review in the *Adkins* case had provided that the minimum wage provided should be adequate to meet the cost of living and to maintain women in good health and morals. This standard, the Court had held, amounted to a confiscation of the property of the employer to the extent that such a wage exceeded the value of the services an employee rendered.

In the *Morehead* case (1936), counsel for New York had sought to distinguish the *Adkins* case (1923) on the grounds that New York's minimum wage statute did not contain a provision similar to the one held confiscatory by the Court in the *Adkins* case. The Court held by a vote of five to four that the New York minimum wage was invalid on liberty of contract grounds, reiterating the principles of *Adkins* v. *Children's Hospital*. In the *Schechter* (1935) and *Carter* (1936) cases, the Court had held that the federal government could not regulate wages and other conditions of employment because they were "local" in nature, yet in the *Morehead* case the Court was saying that the states could not validly regulate wages either, thus creating a constitutional "no-man's-land" in which both the federal government and the states were forbidden to enter.

The *Morehead* case (1936) also appeared to indicate that liberty of contract was a healthy and viable constitutional doctrine as far as a majority of the Court was concerned, a circumstance that might mean that the doctrine of the *Adair* (1908) and *Coppage* (1915) cases was also still viable. As a result of the Court's 1936 decisions, especially in the *Carter* case, the NLRB began to consider the necessity of reducing its operations in manufacturing and production industries because such activities would only give the workers in those industries false hopes in regard to the protection of their right to organize under the NLRA. One staff member of the Board suggested, however, that the NLRB continue to hold hearings in production industries even though its jurisdiction to do so was probably invalid, since such hearings would aid unionization drives in production industries. He said that the:

> . . . NLRB at present sits on its triple throne, a bit like the church shorn of its right to prosecute and hang. Despite the loss of temporal power, NLRB can still thunder from the pulpit and excommunicate from the congregation of the righteous. That comforts the flock, disconcerts the heathen,—and marks down the latter against the day of wrath to come. Relegate metaphysics to the Supreme Tribunal, and get on with good works?

The Board instead issued instructions to its staff in May 1936, to reduce hearings in doubtful industries and to subject new cases "to more careful scrutiny than they have been in the past." First preference as far as hearings were concerned, the Board ordered, should be given to cases involving interstate transportation and communication, since the latter businesses were clearly in interstate commerce and if the NLRA were valid at all, it could perhaps be applied to such clearly interstate industries. The staff was also advised that this reduction of the scope of the NLRB's jurisdiction might well shake the confidence of labor in the Board, but the staff should do all it could to retain this labor confidence.

LABOR'S CIVIL WAR

The concern of the Board with maintaining labor's confidence was well justified since in 1935 organized labor split into two warring camps, thus adding another problem to the Board's burden. The issue of craft versus industrial unionism had threatened the cohesiveness of the union movement since the beginning of the New Deal. John L. Lewis, president of the United Mine Workers, was the acknowledged leader of those in the AFL who advocated vigorous organizing drives in the mass production industries using the industrial form of union organization. Instead of attempting to parcel out employees in these industries to the various craft unions, Lewis and his supporters argued that the only effective method of organizing the mass production industries was to organize all the workers in such industries into one union. Lewis was particularly concerned with the lack of unionization in the steel industry, since he believed that as long as steel remained unorganized the UMW was threatened. The steel industry was also regarded as the leading anti-union industry in the country, and the industrial union faction in the AFL knew that steel had to be organized if organizing drives were to succeed in other industries.

In the 1934 AFL convention, President Tighe of the Amalgamated Association of Iron, Steel and Tin Workers reported that of the steel workers recruited by his union from 1933 to 1934, only 5,300 still remained in the union. This led Lewis to propose that the organization of the steel industry be taken out of Tighe's hands. The convention agreed and resolved to issue charters for the organization of all mass production industries, and at the "earliest possible date inaugurate, manage, promote and conduct a campaign of organization in the steel industry." The convention determined, however, that the workers organized in the mass production industries would be parceled out to the old line AFL craft unions according to the jobs they performed. Experience with this approach, however, proved discouraging in attempts to organize the auto and rubber industries.

When the AFL convention met in 1935, only three months after the passage of the NLRA, the problem of how to organize the mass production workers was still unresolved. The majority of the resolutions committee again proposed a resolution similar to the one adopted in 1934 on this question, but a minority of the committee argued that in the "great mass production industries and those in which the workers are composite mechanics, specialized and engaged in classes of work which do not qualify them for craft-union membership, industrial organization is the only solution. . . ." The AFL now faced a clear-cut decision on the issue that would split the labor movement for twenty years. Eloquent as usual, John L. Lewis urged the convention to support the minority report in favor of industrial union organization of the mass production workers, imploring the convention to heed "this cry from Macedonia that comes from the hearts of men. Organize the unorganized and in doing this make the A.F. of L. the greatest instrument that has ever been forged to befriend the cause of humanity and champion human rights." The industrial union faction at the convention again pointed to the steel industry as the leading example of the failure of craft unionism in the mass production industries. Phillip Murray, a vice president of the UMW, thus told the convention that 8,000 workers at the Jones & Laughlin plant at Aliquippa had organized themselves into an independent union and were refusing to accept craft union charters from the AFL.

The majority of the convention was unmoved and the majority report of the resolutions committee was adopted. The following day the industrial union faction, led by Lewis, Sidney Hillman of the Amalgamated Clothing Workers, and David Dubinsky of the International Ladies' Garment Workers Union, met and planned the Committee for Industrial Organization. In January 1936 the executive committee of the AFL condemned the CIO and later expelled the unions participating in the CIO from the AFL. The unity of the American labor movement was at an end.

The split in the labor movement ultimately caused difficulties for the NLRB. The time and effort spent by the AFL and the CIO fighting one another could have better served the cause of labor if expended in support of the Board and the NLRA. The NLRA provided that the Board would determine the appropriate bargaining unit in which to hold representation elections, whether it was the "employer unit, craft unit, plant unit, or other unit." In determining the appropriate bargaining units in industry, the NLRB was often confronted with choosing units that would favor either the AFL or the CIO. The AFL finally concluded that the Board was favoring the CIO in such decisions. By 1937 the AFL was thus denouncing the NLRB as having "disrupted tried and tested principles of collective bargaining" and as having "brought turmoil and havoc into industrial relations, usurped the prerogatives of the courts essential to our democratic form of government, and jeopardized industrial freedom and initiative." Fortunately for the Board, however, the most severe difficulties caused by labor's civil war came after the crucial period of 1935 to 1937. During this period the Board was able to secure cooperation from organized labor in not pressing cases upon it that were not sound from a constitutional standpoint.

THE NLRB AND THE
LA FOLLETTE COMMITTEE

The final major problem faced by the NLRB in defending the NLRA during this period was the problem of public relations. The press was overwhelmingly hostile, especially after the Board began to assume jurisdiction in newspaper and press cases in 1936. As Malcolm Ross, the NLRB's Director of Information, wrote later, during the 1935 to 1937 period the Board "in three words, caught unmitigated hell." The Board found a powerful ally in its attempt to counteract the unfavorable publicity it received when the La Follette Committee was created by the Senate in June 1936. A staff member of the NLRB, Heber Blankenhorn, conceived of a congressional investigating committee as the best device by which to counteract the unfavorable publicity the Board was receiving and to expose the obstructionist tactics facing the Board inspired by such groups as the Liberty League and the NAM. The committee concentrated on the denial to workers of freedom of speech, assembly, and the right to organize by employers.

The La Follette Committee's investigations, which turned up frightening information in regard to the extent to which American industry utilized labor spies and strongarm tactics of intimidation against workers to prevent unionization, was of the utmost importance to the NLRB during the crucial period of its battle for survival. When the Board was to an extent paralyzed by injunctions and was reducing its jurisdiction because of the *Carter* case (1936), a substantial part of the NLRB staff devoted their time to aiding the La Follette Committee. And when the injunction suit attack on the Board reached its height, one staff member suggested that the Board present its cases before the La Follette Committee when it was enjoined from holding hearings. "It ought not to take more than one or two such hearings," he said, "to make companies hesitant about rushing to courts for injunctions, at least as far as hearings go."

The cooperation of the La Follette Committee could not overcome the NLRB's constitutional difficulties. Those difficulties could only be solved by the Board's successful defense of the NLRA in test cases before the Supreme Court. Despite the ordeal the Board experienced during the dark days of 1935 to 1937, it had managed to retain control of the litigation testing the validity of the NLRA, and the Board initiated proceedings in those cases that appeared to offer the best chance of successfully defending the NLRA before the Court. By 1937 five cases were pending before the Supreme Court in which the fate of the NLRA would be decided. The key case among those five test cases was *NLRB* v. *Jones & Laughlin Steel Corporation,* a case whose history we shall now examine.

❧ 4 ❧

THE
JONES & LAUGHLIN
CASE

━━━◄◆►━━━

The National Labor Relations Board might have delayed a test of the NLRA before the Supreme Court as long as possible. This had been the strategy of the Justice Department in regard to the National Industrial Recovery Act, a measure about which there had been grave constitutional doubts, just as there were in regard to the NLRA. The result of the Justice Department's failure to select a strong case upon which to test the validity of the NIRA had of course been disastrous. The *Schechter* case (1935) was a notably weak case from the government's standpoint.

THE STRATEGY OF THE NLRB

The members of the NLRB were acutely aware of the *Schechter* case (1935) disaster, and from the beginning rejected a strategy like that used by the Justice Department. As NLRB Chairman Warren Madden said later, the:

. . . Board was resolved that the cases which reached the Supreme Court should, if possible, be impressive cases which involved important and significant enterprises. We were aware that the Supreme Court case in which the NIRA had been held invalid had become popularly known as the "sick chicken case." We did not intend to allow ourselves to be maneuvered into a litigation in which we would be asserting that it was necessary to draw upon the vast arsenal of the national power in order to bring under control a situation which could, in fact, be quieted with a pop-gun.

The "Sick Chicken" case haunted the Board. When some of its early proceedings against employers involved companies named "Kiddie Cover," and "Infant Sox," the Board lived in "dread of finding ourselves in the Supreme Court with such cases."

Because of the *Schechter* case (1935) the NLRB adopted a strategy of carefully selecting cases upon which the NLRA could best be defended before the Supreme Court. The Board also adopted the position that since the NLRA was applicable to any business that could be reached by Congress under the Commerce Clause the act was valid, but that in particular cases the Board might apply it to businesses beyond the scope of congressional power. The NLRB maintained that while the courts might hold the act to have been invalidly applied, they could not hold the act to be unconstitutional. The Board hoped that the ultimate scope of the NLRA in terms of the businesses to which it could be validly applied would be determined on a case by case basis as the courts reviewed particular applications of the act by the Board.

An examination of Supreme Court decisions in regard to labor and labor relations revealed that the strongest precedent in favor of the NLRA was the *Texas & New Orleans Railroad* case (1930) in which the Court had sustained the Railway Labor Act of 1926. If Congress could validly protect the right of workers to organize free from employer interference on interstate railroads, it followed that the NLRA might be valid when applied to a business in interstate commerce as similar as possible to an interstate railroad. The initial strategy of the NLRB was therefore to proceed against a business clearly interstate in nature and to seek a Supreme Court ruling on the validity of the NLRA in such a case.

The first proceeding brought by the Board was against the Pennsylvania Greyhound Lines, Inc. Pennsylvania Greyhound Lines was a bus company engaged in the interstate transportation of passengers, an activity clearly in interstate commerce and as analogous to the activity of an interstate railroad as possible. The company was charged with dominating a company union and with discharging employees who were union members, both actions being in violation of the NLRA. The NLRB held hearings in the *Pennsylvania Greyhound Lines* case in early October 1935, and in December it announced its decision that the company was guilty of unfair labor practices. The Board ordered the company to cease and desist from such unfair labor practices and to reinstate the employees discharged for their union membership. "Operated as an integrated system through traffic agreements, interline tariffs, connecting schedules and joint advertising," the Board said in description of the company's operations, "the Greyhound Lines presents striking similarities to our national railroad systems."

The Board also petitioned the Court of Appeals for the Third Circuit for an enforcement order in December, believing it had an interstate commerce case as closely resembling the *Texas & New Orleans Railroad* case (1930) as possible. It is clear that the Board expected to test the validity of the NLRA before the Supreme Court in the *Pennsylvania Greyhound Lines* case, but this initial strategy of the Board aborted when the Third Circuit Court of Appeals continued to delay deciding the case either for or against the Board, thus blocking any appeal to the Supreme Court. Warren Madden thus explained later that because the Court of Appeals was "unwilling to be the first to face the constitutional questions, [it] delayed its decision so long that [the *Pennsylvania Greyhound Lines* case] lost its place in our design for Supreme Court review."

In its search for a strong interstate commerce case the Board's luck changed for the better when the Associated Press fired Morris Watson, one of its star reporters in New York, for reasons that were clearly due to his membership in the American Newspaper Guild. The AP was clearly operating in interstate commerce since it utilized interstate telegraph and telephone wires to transmit news to its members. The Board ultimately charged the AP with unfair labor practices under the NLRA, and despite a strenuous defense of the AP by its counsel, John W. Davis of the Liberty League, the Board secured an important victory when the Court of Appeals for the Second Circuit upheld the act as it applied to the AP, relying primarily on the *Texas & New Orleans Railroad* case (1930).

The NLRB's victory in the *Associated Press* case meant that for the first time the NLRA's application to a business had withstood a test in the court of appeals. The Board at last had its interstate commerce case, but victory in the court of appeals meant that it lost control over the case insofar as an appeal to the Supreme Court was concerned, since a petition for a writ of certiorari would now have to be initiated by John W. Davis and the AP. Given Davis' views on the constitutionality of the NLRA it could be expected that an appeal to the Supreme Court would be made as a matter of course, but the decision was his and not the Board's.

Although the NLRB was successful in winning a significant victory in the *Associated Press* case, the crucial test of the NLRA would come when it was applied to businesses whose activities were not interstate commerce per se. The Supreme Court's insistence upon the direct-indirect effects formula as a fundamental constitutional doctrine in such cases as the

Schechter (1935) and *Carter Coal Company* (1936) cases cast grave doubts upon the validity of the NLRA as applied to manufacturing or production enterprises. The Board nonetheless felt that under the stream of commerce cases the act might be validly applied to at least some manufacturing companies if the operations of those companies could be demonstrated to be quite similar to the factual situations the Court had had before it in the stream of commerce cases. While seeking out a strong interstate commerce case, and having found one in the *Associated Press* case, the NLRB also proceeded against several manufacturing companies, despite the grave doubts that such proceedings were valid under the Commerce Clause.

THE *JONES & LAUGHLIN* CASE

The continued anti-unionism of the Jones & Laughlin Steel Corporation at its Aliquippa plant ultimately presented the NLRB with the key case for testing the validity of the NLRA as applied to production enterprises. Like the rest of the steel industry Jones & Laughlin had installed an employee representation plan (company union) during the NIRA period, and it had paid the expenses of some of its employees to journey to Washington to oppose the NLRA during the Senate hearings on the act. This group of five employees had been led by William Westlake, an employee representative under the employee representation plan. Westlake was defeated for reelection as a representative because of his testimony against the NLRA. In June 1935, when the elections for representatives under the employee representation plan were held, Harry Phillips, the president of the Aliquippa local of the Amalgamated Association of Iron, Steel and Tin Workers, urged the Jones & Laughlin workers to boycott the elections. The company countered this by applying a great deal of pressure on its employees to vote in the elections. The regional director for the NLRB, Clinton S. Golden, reported to the Board that he was "advised that the Company went to considerable effort to get the employees to vote, that Company police were sent to the homes of the workers and there threatened them with discharge unless they did participate in the election, and that in fact some twenty odd employees were dismissed for refusing to participate." Golden sent an NLRB field representative to investigate the situation in Aliquippa, but Golden warned him that he regarded the situation as explosive and that "there is a very real possibility of trouble developing" at Aliquippa.

Trouble did develop the following month when the company began to discharge union leaders, giving as reasons rather negligible infractions of company rules. The first to go was Martin Dunn, a charter member of the union and a crane operator, who was discharged on July 9 for leaving the key to his crane on a bench in violation of company rules. Next came Harry Phillips, the president of the union, who was discharged for failure to answer a whistle while he was in the restroom, and a few days later, Angelo Volpe, the union's vice-president, was discharged for operating his crane on the basis of head signals from his helper rather than the required hand signals. Several more of the union's leaders were discharged over the months from July through January: Domenic Brandy, the leader of Aliquippa's Italian community; George Royal Boyer, a leader of the Negro workers; Ronald Cox, a charter union member; Martin Gerstner, financial secretary and charter member of the union; Angelo Razzano, who had signed up fifteen hundred workers for the union; and Eli Bozich, a leader of the Croatian workers and a charter union member.

In answer to complaints by the union, the company said that the "cases have all been fairly investigated and the men were discharged for cause." Accordingly a charge of unfair labor practices was filed by the local with the NLRB on January 28, 1936. Jones & Laughlin immediately secured Earl F.

Reed as its counsel. Clinton Golden began to worry about the prospective hearing on the discharges:

> I am sure you realize that Jones & Laughlin is one of the major units in steel industry, that Earl Reed is their attorney, and that the case is bound to be fought vigorously by the Company. While our Regional Attorney is a bright and intelligent chap, he has been out of college only a little over a year. I am inclined to believe that this case may be one of the most important ones coming before the Board, and I would personally feel a lot safer if he had some assistance on handling same.

Golden also suggested that expert testimony be introduced by the Board in the hearing.

Reed was busy elsewhere at the time the Board's complaint was issued and requested a postponement of the hearing that was scheduled for February. Reed's request was granted, but the Board was able to extract a *quid pro quo*. Thanking the Board for the postponement, Reed assured the Board that he had "asked them at the plant to be particularly careful that nothing occurs to change the situation during the month of adjournment, and it is also understood that we will not ask for any injunction against the holding of the hearing, although our appearance may be a special appearance." On February 20 Reed again requested that the hearing be postponed, but this time his request was refused, and a week later the Board announced that it would come from Washington to Pittsburgh to hear the case.

At the hearing the Board's attorney introduced evidence purporting to show the interstate nature of Jones & Laughlin's operations, but Reed objected to any evidence on the merits of the case before he obtained a determination on the jurisdictional issue. He put on company officials who testified that only raw materials, such as iron ore, limestone, and coal, entered the Aliquippa plant and then those materials were utilized to manufacture steel products that were then shipped to consumers across the country. Reed's point was obviously to demonstrate for the record that while raw materials entered the Aliquippa plant in interstate commerce, their interstate movement ceased completely once they were delivered at the plant, and interstate commerce did not resume until after the steel products that were manufactured in the plant began their journey to interstate markets. The activities in the plant, and the labor relations in regard to them, Reed was arguing, consisted entirely of production, a local activity that was not interstate commerce. Following this testimony Reed therefore moved to dismiss the unfair labor practice charges on the grounds that the NLRB lacked jurisdiction over manufacturing enterprises, including those at Jones & Laughlin's Aliquippa plant.

MR. REED: That is all the evidence that respondent has on the question of the interstate commerce feature of the case, and we move to dismiss, on the ground that the evidence adduced by the Board and also that adduced by respondent, shows conclusively, within the decisions of the courts, that the business of the respondent is not interstate commerce, and any labor controversy, therefore, would not be within the jurisdiction of the Board. Further, the complaint only complains of matters of hiring or discharging employees, which is a matter that is not interstate commerce, even if it related to any agency in interstate commerce, and it seems clear to us that there is no jurisdiction in this case.

MR. MADDEN: It would be very interesting, Mr. Reed, to hear you argue this question, but I suppose you do not care to do it, and I doubt whether we can take the time to do it. We are quite definitely committed to the doctrine that an enterprise such as has been shown, both by the government's evidence and by your own evidence here, is in a situation where its labor relations do affect interstate commerce, within the meaning of the Act, and so your motion to dismiss is denied.

MR. REED: With respect to the specific complaints relating to employees, the respondent takes the position that it is the sole judge of the right to hire and fire, and that it is not subject to the Board in that respect, and therefore, declines to offer any testimony on that subject and withdraws from the hearing. We will stand on our legal position that the Board has no jurisdiction in this case.

The evidence introduced by the Board and the company had shown Jones & Laughlin to be the fourth largest steel producer in the United States with gross assets valued at more than 181 million dollars and with over 22,000 employees, 10,000 of whom were employed at the Aliquippa plant. The company was shown to be a completely integrated steel manufacturer, owning iron ore, coal, and limestone properties in Michigan, Minnesota, Pennsylvania, and West Virginia and owning railroad and river barge subsidiaries. Approximately 75 percent of Jones & Laughlin's products were shipped out of the state of Pennsylvania to its subsidiaries scattered across the country. In opposition to Reed's position, the Board thus argued that the Jones & Laughlin Aliquippa plant was the focal point or throat through which an ever-recurring stream or flow of interstate commerce in raw materials and finished steel products passed, and that a strike in the Aliquippa plant would have a direct, substantial, and immediate impact upon interstate commerce.

Following Reed's withdrawal, the discharged men were called. They testified on the history of intimidation in Aliquippa and their own discharges by Jones & Laughlin. The discharged workers testified to continuous harassment of union members by Jones & Laughlin foremen and police. Martin Gerstner testified that company agents guarded his "house twenty-four hours a day, and the employment agent who was up there for weeks, sitting in the doorway to check every man that went in and out." Another of the discharged workers testified that he committed a minor infraction of the company rules, and a foreman immediately reported it by telephone to his superiors and asked, "Is that enough?" The worker was told that Jones & Laughlin would not tolerate his falling behind in the rent on his company house and merchants would refuse him credit if he persisted in union activities. Jones & Laughlin, he was told, had "determined to fight this case to the highest court, and they would close the plant down and throw the key in the river before they would recognize an outside union. . . ."

Other discharged employees were told that the "union is no good in this town. This is a company town." And one union member who was discharged later testified about his being questioned in regard to the *Schechter* decision (1935) by the Supreme Court. A Jones & Laughlin superintendent had asked him, "What do you think of the N.R.A. now? Well, it is overruled, isn't it?" The worker pointed out that the National Labor Relations Act was pending before Congress, but the superintendent replied that the "Supreme Court is going to overrule that." The worker replied, "Well, let them do what they please. We are organized anyhow. We started to organize in 1934 and we keep on going."

The hearing ended on March 14 but was reopened in Washington for additional testimony from April 2 through 8. Unlike business groups during the 1930s, the NLRB could not pursue the defensive tactic of relying entirely on the established interpretation of the Constitution but rather had to pursue aggressive tactics if it was to succeed in the courts. In this sense, the NLRB was in essentially the same position in the 1930s that business corporations had occupied during the post-Civil War period. Like corporations during that period, it was vital from the Board's standpoint to have as much favorable nonlegal material in the record of the *Jones & Laughlin* case as possible, in order to offset its disadvantages in terms of the prevailing constitutional doctrine. It was for the purpose of securing a more convincing record, therefore, that the Board reopened the hearing in Washington during April.

The evidence introduced in the Washington hearing was in the nature of testimony by numerous experts in labor problems covering the whole gamut of labor relations in the United States. By this testimony and by statistical evidence, the

Board sought to demonstrate that: (1) a substantial proportion of the strikes in industry were caused by the refusal of employers to recognize the right of workers to organize and bargain collectively; (2) where this right was recognized by employers, labor relations were generally more peaceful, as in the garment and printing industries; (3) there were many precedents historically for federal intervention in labor disputes; (4) the steel industry, since the formation of the large integrated combinations, had denied the right to organize to its employees; (5) and strikes in most manufacturing and production industries, and thus the steel industry, drastically affected the flow of goods in interstate commerce. The addition of this evidence to the record in the case was, in short, the use of the Brandeis brief technique on a grand scale and was the Board's answer to the briefs of the Liberty League, the NAM, and other employer associations purporting to demonstrate the NLRA's unconstitutionality. The material from this hearing was issued in summarized pamphlet form by the Board "for the information and assistance of the courts and others who may desire to have in convenient form some of the learning which has been gathered during the years in the various fields covered by the witnesses."

On April 9 the Board issued its decision finding Jones & Laughlin guilty of unfair labor practices and ordering it to cease and desist from such practices and to reinstate the discharged employees with back pay for time lost. The Board said that:

The ramifications of the Jones & Laughlin Steel Corporation are . . . as broadly extended as the nation itself. It is impossible to isolate the operations of the Works in Pittsburgh and Aliquippa or to consider them as detached, separate—"local"—phenomena. These Works might be likened to a heart of a self-contained, highly integrated body. They draw their raw materials from Michigan, Minnesota, West Virginia and Pennsylvania in part through arteries and by means controlled by respondent; they transform materials and then pump them out to all parts of the nation through the vast mechanism which the respondent has elaborated.

The Board's legal staff had in the meantime been circuit shopping in an effort to find the most favorable court in which to bring a petition of enforcement. The Third Circuit Court of Appeals, which would have been the logical court in which to file such a petition, had been sitting on the *Pennsylvania Greyhound Lines* case and it seemed unlikely that the court would be any more disposed to deal quickly with the *Jones & Laughlin* case. The NLRB thus searched elsewhere for a court of appeals in which to file its enforcement petition. Robert Watts, an experienced trial lawyer recruited by the Board to handle its litigation as Associate General Counsel, telegraphed Charles Fahy from the field suggesting that Fahy "consider seriously petition to enforce in the Fifth Circuit instead of Second or Third. Believe would secure early argument and favorable ruling which would greatly assist general situation." The NLRA required that an enterprise against which a petition of enforcement was sought had to be conducting business within the circuit where the petition was filed. Jones & Laughlin owned a structural steel fabricating shop in New Orleans, which was within the Fifth Circuit. The Board ordered a regional attorney to discover "whether the company does business in Louisiana only through its subsidiary, or whether it does business directly in its own name. Will you make every effort to get us that information, since the Board may desire to bring its court case in the Fifth Circuit. . . ." It was confirmed on March 21 that Jones & Laughlin did business in Louisiana in its own name, and on April 9 the Board filed a petition of enforcement in the Fifth Circuit Court of Appeals in New Orleans.

Arguments were delayed to June 1 on the request of the company's counsel, and at the same time the NLRB asked the court for more time for oral argument. Robert Watts requested a regional attorney to ask for at least two hours for oral arguments because of the case's "importance and because of the somewhat complex constitutional questions raised. . . . At the same time, I am most anxious that we shall not jeopardize our present friendly relations with the Court. With that in mind, use the utmost courtesy and deference in contacting the Court and present our request as largely our own honest feeling. . . ." The request was granted, and Watts argued the case on June 1, reporting to Fahy that it went "very well with the Court appearing friendly . . . ," but appearances were deceiving, since the court denied the Board's petition in an opinion announced on June 15. Relying on the *Carter Coal Company* case (1936), the court held that:

> . . . petition must be denied, because, under the facts found by the Board and shown by the evidence, the Board has no jurisdiction over a labor dispute between employer and employees touching the discharge of the laborers in a steel plant, who were engaged only in manufacture. The Constitution does not vest in the federal government the power to regulate the relations as such of employer and employee in production or manufacture.

The *Carter Coal Company* decision (1936) and the direct-indirect effects formula thus appeared to be an impenetrable barrier to the Board's assertion of jurisdiction over manufacturing and production enterprises, and the Board uniformly lost such cases in the courts of appeals. The *Carter* case thus led one attorney defending several manufacturing companies, against which the Board had proceeded, to write to the Board demanding that it obey the Constitution and dismiss the cases. The attorney pointed out that he had raised:

> . . . issues with respect to the National Labor Relations act which were decided by the Supreme Court the day before yesterday [in the *Carter* case]. . . . It now must be obvious to you, that labor conditions in the manufacturing industries are not subject to regulation by the Federal Government under the commerce clause and due process amendment to the Constitution, and that under this decision the National Labor Relations Act is unconstitutional. . . . [His clients were entitled] to now have you say that they

have not been acting in violation of any valid law. We, therefore, request, in view of the great publicity given by you to these charges when you instituted them and again when you found these companies guilty, that you now publicly dismiss these cases.

The Board replied emphatically that it intended:

. . . to proceed with the cases to which you refer as it has in the past. . . . You undoubtedly realized that the [*Carter* case] affected the [Bituminous Coal Act], and had no legal effect on the Act under which the Board operates. We are sure that you also realized that the recent decision of the Supreme Court was based on the facts before it, and not on anything involved in cases before the Board, nor on the statute under which the Board operates.

Despite the fact that the *Carter* case (1936) seemed to be the death knell of its jurisdiction over manufacturing and production enterprises, the Board thus fostered other manufacturing cases along toward the Supreme Court in addition to the *Jones & Laughlin* case.

THE COMPANION CASES

In 1937 the *Jones & Laughlin* case was joined in the Supreme Court by the *Fruehauf Trailer Company* case and the *Friedman-Harry Marks Clothing Company* case, both involving manufacturing companies as did the *Jones & Laughlin* case. The Fruehauf Trailer Company was a medium size manufacturer of truck trailers in Detroit, while the Friedman-Harry Marks Clothing Company was a relatively small clothing manufacturer in Richmond, Virginia. In both cases, as in the *Jones & Laughlin* case, the Board argued that these companies utilized raw materials shipped in interstate commerce and in turn shipped their products in interstate commerce. A strike in either, in the Board's view, would have a substantial impact or effect upon interstate commerce. The courts of appeals, however, denied enforcement petitions in both the *Fruehauf* and *Friedman-Harry Marks* cases, relying as in the *Jones & Laughlin* case upon the doctrine that manufacturing was not interstate commerce and affected interstate commerce only indirectly.

The fifth and final case that tested the validity of the NLRA before the Supreme Court was the *Washington, Virginia and Maryland Coach Company* case. This company was a small bus company that operated buses between Virginia and Washington, D.C. The company had discharged eighteen of its eighty employees for union membership and had been proceeded against by the Board. The Board had won the *Washington, Virginia and Maryland Coach Company* case in the Fourth Circuit Court of Appeals since the company was clearly operating in interstate commerce despite its small size. The company appealed to the Supreme Court and there the case joined the *Associated Press* case as a case involving the application of the NLRA to a clearly interstate business.

Although there had been constant contact between the Board and Solicitor General Stanley Reed's office on the status of the Board's litigation, the Board had controlled the selection of cases in which to file complaints and those in which petitions of enforcement would be filed. As the cases passed the court of appeals level, however, the Solicitor General assumed the ultimate power of selection as to cases with which to approach the Court. Because the Board's original strategy for a quick test of the NLRA in the *Pennsylvania Greyhound Lines* case had gone awry, two of its manufacturing cases, the *Fruehauf* and *Jones & Laughlin* cases, were decided in the courts of appeals before an interstate commerce case had reached that stage. Since the constitutionality of the Board's manufacturing jurisdiction was extremely doubtful, the Board was forced to hold these manufacturing cases back until an interstate commerce case that could accompany them to the Supreme Court was brought out of the courts of appeals. In losing its manufacturing cases in the courts of appeals, the Board re-

tained the discretion as to whether petitions for writs of certiorari would be filed in such cases, but in its interstate commerce cases it was forced to wait upon the decisions of the
companies involved as to whether or not an appeal would be
taken to the Supreme Court.

Following the Fifth Circuit Court of Appeals decision in the
Jones & Laughlin case on June 17, Charles Fahy had written
Robert Watts pointing out that they must find out how much
time was allowed for filing a petition for a writ of certiorari
and "whether we should ask for a rehearing from a tactical
standpoint in order to keep the case alive in its present status
for a longer period of time until our other Circuit Court situations have cleared up and we will have more decisions to consider as a basis for approaching the Supreme Court." It was
decided that a petition for a rehearing should be filed, in
order to extend the time available to the Board for deciding
whether to appeal the case to the Supreme Court. Similarly,
after the *Fruehauf* case was lost in the Sixth Circuit Court of
Appeals on June 30, 1936, Fahy telegraphed the regional attorney that it was "possible we will petition the Supreme Court
for a writ of certiorari in the *Fruehauf* case so we desire motion filed for stay of mandate, although it is not desired that
motion state that certiorari will be applied for if it is possible
to avoid such commitment at this time. . . ." Both the *Fruehauf* and *Jones & Laughlin* cases were thus kept alive pending
the decision of an interstate commerce case in the courts of appeals and the appeal of such a case to the Supreme Court.

In the *Associated Press* case, John W. Davis approached the
Board on July 20 and requested its agreement for a stay of the
mandate of the court of appeals for forty days to allow time
for the filing of a petition for a writ of certiorari in the Supreme Court. The Board was thus assured of obtaining review of a strong interstate commerce case before the Supreme
Court. "I think the *Associated Press* case is a very good one to
go to the Supreme Court," Charles Fahy wrote, "and I am per-

fectly willing, from the standpoint of the Board, not to object to a stay of the order in exchange for an agreement by the Associated Press that within a definite period of time it will apply for review by the Supreme Court." Fahy met with Solicitor General Stanley Reed on July 29 and reported that he was sure that "this is also his position, although I cannot speak positively as to this for the reason that there has been no occasion for him to make a categorical statement." Davis was informed, therefore, that the Board would not object to a stay nor would it oppose a petition for a writ of certiorari, "subject to the approval of the Solicitor General," and on September 14 the Associated Press filed its petition for a writ of certiorari with the Supreme Court.

With the *Associated Press* case thus pending before the Court, the Board began to move again on its manufacturing cases. In addition to the *Fruehauf* and *Jones & Laughlin* cases, the *Friedman-Harry Marks* case, decided on the same day as the *Associated Press* case, was being considered as a possible test case. On August 1, Fahy informed a regional attorney that the "Department of Justice desires us to print the proceedings in the Second Circuit in the *Friedman-Harry Marks* case to have the matter in condition for filing with the Supreme Court a petition for certiorari." Petitions for writs of certiorari in the three manufacturing cases were drafted by the Board, but no final decision on their filing had been made by August 22. Robert Watts submitted the drafts to the Solicitor General's office on that date, stating his "understanding that no final action will be taken in filing any of these petitions until the return of Mr. Fahy and further discussion between him and the Solicitor General on the subject." After John W. Davis filed his appeal in the *Associated Press* case, however, the decision was soon made by the Solicitor General and the Board to appeal the manufacturing cases, and petitions for writs of certiorari were filed in the manufacturing cases on September 30. The *Washington, Virginia and Mary-*

land Coach Company case was not decided in the court of appeals until October 6, but in that case the company immediately appealed the court of appeals decision, supplying the fifth and final case testing the validity of the NLRA before the Supreme Court.

On October 26, 1936, the Supreme Court granted the petitions for certiorari in the *Associated Press* and *Washington, Virginia and Maryland Coach Company* cases, and on November 9, it granted the government's petitions in the *Jones & Laughlin, Fruehauf,* and *Friedman-Harry Marks* cases. With these five cases, the NLRB presented the Court with the broadest possible range of choices in determining the validity of the National Labor Relations Act. If the Court decided that the act could be validly applied only to businesses whose activities were clearly interstate in nature, then it could sustain the validity of the act in the *Associated Press* and *Washington, Virginia and Maryland Coach Company* cases, but hold that the act had been invalidly applied by the Board in the manufacturing cases. If the Court should decide that the Commerce Clause did not absolutely prohibit legislation regulating the labor relations of manufacturing enterprises, but that such regulation was valid in those situations where strikes in manufacturing enterprises would substantially affect interstate commerce, then the Court could look at each of the manufacturing cases and determine in which of them the act had been validly applied. The Court could thus determine that a strike in the Jones & Laughlin Aliquippa plant would affect commerce so substantially as to justify congressional regulation, while holding that strikes in the Fruehauf Trailer Company or Friedman-Harry Marks Clothing Company would not affect commerce sufficiently to justify such regulation; or the Court could hold that the NLRB could be validly applied to large and medium sized manufacturers, like Jones & Laughlin and the Fruehauf Company, but not to a small manufacturer like the Friedman-Harry Marks Clothing Company. A maximum victory for the Board would of course occur if the Court upheld the application of the NLRA not only in the interstate commerce cases but also in all of the manufacturing cases, an outcome that in the fall of 1936 seemed highly unlikely. Haunting the Board in each of the cases, however, was the possibility that the *Texas & New Orleans Railroad* case (1930) had not in fact buried the doctrine of the *Adair* (1908) and *Coppage* (1915) cases, and if this was so, the NLRA would be declared unconstitutional in each case on the grounds that it interfered with the liberty of contract protected by the Fifth Amendment.

The cases testing the validity of the NLRA were scheduled to be heard by the Supreme Court in the spring of 1937, but by that time a series of events had begun that would ultimately overshadow the careful work that was proceeding in the offices of the NLRB and the Justice Department on the five cases. Franklin Roosevelt had been reelected in November 1936, carrying every state but Maine and Vermont and receiving the largest popular vote in history. In his first term he had seen almost every major part of his New Deal program fall before the constitutional strictures of the Supreme Court. And in 1936 cases challenging two more major pieces of New Deal legislation, the National Labor Relations Act and the Social Security Act, were moving toward the Court. At the first cabinet meeting following the election Roosevelt therefore raised the issue of what to do about the Court. He was soon setting in motion plans that when announced would precipitate the gravest executive-judicial conflict since the Civil War and make the decisions in the NLRA cases a crucial turning point in this broader conflict.

~§ 5 §~

THE CRISIS OF 1937

<hr>

On January 15, 1937, President Roosevelt wrote his long-time friend and ardent supporter, Professor Felix Frankfurter of the Harvard Law School. At the end of a letter that dealt with other matters, Roosevelt warned Frankfurter that "I may give you an awful shock in about two weeks. Even if you do not agree, suspend final judgment and I will tell you the story." Frankfurter replied, asking if Roosevelt was "trying to find out how well I can sit on top of a Vesuvius by giving me notice that 'an awful shock' is in store for me 'in about two weeks?' Well, I shall try to hold my patience and fortify my capacity to withstand 'an awful shock,' but you certainly tease my curiosity when you threaten me with something with which I may not agree. That, certainly, would be a great surprise." Roosevelt was hinting to Frankfurter in regard to the "court-packing" plan that he proposed to Congress on February 5. The court-packing plan asked Congress to authorize the President to appoint to any federal court, including the Supreme Court, an additional judge for each judge who failed to retire within six months after reaching the retirement age of seventy. Under the plan, the number of additional Justices was limited to six for the Supreme Court and to fifty additional judges for the lower federal courts.

As early as 1935 Roosevelt had remarked to his Secretary of Labor, Frances Perkins, that he had been President for two years without an appointment to the Supreme Court. "That's unusual, I am told," he said. "What the Court needs is some Roosevelt appointments. Then we might get a good decision out of them." But Roosevelt had not yet had an appointment to the Court by 1937, and in the meantime he had seen the major programs of the New Deal, the NIRA, the AAA, the Bituminous Coal Act, and so on, be invalidated one by one by the Court. With the Social Security Act and the National Labor Relations Act soon to be reviewed by the Court, and with new programs in the works, the President felt compelled to move against the Court in order to save the remainder of the New Deal programs. As Roosevelt later said, 1937 thus became the:

> . . . year which was to determine whether the kind of government which the people of the United States had voted for in 1932, 1934, and 1936 was to be permitted by the Supreme Court to function. If it had not been permitted to function as a democracy, it is my reasoned opinion that there would have been great danger that ultimately it might have been compelled to give way to some alien type of government—in the vain hope that the new form of government might be able to give the average men and women the protection and co-operative assistance which they had the right to expect.

Presidents normally may expect a relatively free hand in the selection of Supreme Court Justices,* and as a result the Court

* In the twentieth century, the Senate has failed to confirm only President Hoover's nomination of Parker in 1930, President Johnson's nomination of Abe Fortas as Chief Justice in 1968 and President Nixon's nominations of Clement Haynsworth in 1969 and G. Harrold Carswell in 1970.

usually reflects the political coalition that is capable of electing presidents; and presidential coalitions tend to be dominant over long periods of history with infrequent realignments occurring. The fact that President Roosevelt did not have an opportunity to appoint any members of the Supreme Court from 1933 to 1937 would not under normal conditions have been a factor leading to a severe conflict between the Court and the President. In the 1930s, however, political forces in the United States were undergoing a realignment, and the dominant Republican coalition was rapidly being replaced by a dominant Democratic "Roosevelt" coalition that would control the presidency for a generation to come. The majority of the Court, however, continued to reflect the more conservative values of the predepression presidential coalition, and the fact that Roosevelt did not have any appointments for four years meant that the new, more progressive forces emerging during the depression failed to gain representation on the Court. The result was the invalidation by the Court of the major parts of the New Deal between 1933 and 1937, with the further result that the New Dealers and ultimately the President himself were alienated from the Court. "The bench had been created almost entirely by appointments by conservative Presidents," Roosevelt said later, "and it was now continually passing economic and political judgments, almost month by month, on a liberal program of recovery and reform." In short, the political behavior and thinking of the electorate was undergoing a fundamental change during the 1930s, but the Court did not reflect that change, and the result was a constitutional crisis of major proportions.

The President's proposal that the Court be increased from nine to a maximum of sixteen Justices involved a proposed exercise of power that Congress clearly possesses, since the Constitution does not specify the number of Supreme Court Justices but leaves the number to be set by an act of Congress. The number of Justices had varied from the original six set in

TABLE 1
Number of Supreme Court Justices Authorized by Congress
from 1789–1869

Date Set	No. of Justices	Date Set	No. of Justices
1789	6	1837	9
1801	5	1864	10
1802	6	1866	7*
1807	7	1869	9

* The actual number of Justices on the Court between 1866 and 1869 never fell below eight.

1789 to as high as ten in 1864, but in 1869 the Congress had set the number of Justices at nine and there it had remained. (See Table 1.)

THE COURT IN 1937

The Justices on the Court in 1937 had been appointed by Presidents from William Howard Taft to Herbert Hoover, and six of them were over the retirement age of seventy (Table 2 summarizes the ages, dates of appointment, and partisan affiliations of the Justices).

The senior member of the conservative bloc on the Court was Justice Willis Van Devanter. Born in Indiana, Van Devanter had received his law degree from the University of Cincinnati Law School in 1881. He soon moved to the Wyoming territory where he became prominent as an able attorney and rising politician. After having served as city attorney of Cheyenne and in the territorial legislature, Van Devanter was elected Chief Justice of the Wyoming Supreme Court shortly after Wyoming achieved statehood. He resigned this post after only one year to enter a lucrative law practice defending the great cattle and railroad companies in the region. Van Devanter's political career also continued. He served as Wyoming State Republican Committee Chairman and as a member of the Republican National Committee, working

TABLE 2
The New Deal Justices: 1933–1937

Justice	Year of Birth	Age in 1937	Appointing President	Year of Appointment	Party Affiliation
Brandeis	1856	81	Wilson	1916	Democrat
Van Devanter	1859	78	Taft	1910	Republican
Hughes	1862	75	Hoover	1930	Republican
Sutherland	1862	75	Harding	1922	Republican
McReynolds	1862	75	Wilson	1914	Democrat
Butler	1866	71	Harding	1923	Democrat
Cardozo	1870	67	Hoover	1932	Democrat
Stone	1872	65	Coolidge	1925	Republican
Roberts	1875	62	Hoover	1930	Republican

strenuously in the latter post to defeat William Jennings Bryan in 1896. President McKinley appointed Van Devanter as Assistant Attorney General, and after McKinley's assassination, Theodore Roosevelt appointed him as a judge on the Eighth Circuit Court of Appeals. He was elevated from the Court of Appeals to the Supreme Court by President Taft in 1910.

On the Supreme Court Van Devanter was known for his lucid and careful statements of principles and arguments in conference, and was relied upon heavily by both Chief Justices White and Taft. In 1926 Taft wrote that the:

> . . . value of a judge in conference, especially in such a court as ours, never becomes known except to the members of the court. Now I don't hesitate to say that Mr. Justice Van Devanter is far and away the most valuable man in our court in all these qualities. We have other learned and valuable members, with special knowledge in particular subjects, but Van Devanter has knowledge in every subject that comes before us. . . . Van Devanter exercises more influence, a good deal, than any other member of the court, just because the members of the court know his qualities.

Van Devanter was handicapped, however, more and more as he grew older by what Justice Sutherland called "pen paralysis." When he attempted to write what he had very clearly propounded in conference he simply could not put his ideas in writing. The result was that by the 1930s Chief Justice Hughes assigned fewer opinions to Van Devanter, and was often forced to reassign these cases as the end of a Court term approached and the opinions remained unwritten. Despite this handicap, however, Van Devanter's vote as a member of the conservative bloc continued to be cast against the major programs of the New Deal.

Justice George Sutherland appears to have been the leader of the conservative bloc on the Court during the 1930s. Born in England in 1862, Sutherland's Mormon family emigrated to Utah in 1863. Educated at Brigham Young Academy (later Brigham Young University), Sutherland was taught that the Constitution was a divinely inspired document and he was also exposed to the principles of Herbert Spencer. Herbert Spencer's philosophy was embraced enthusiastically by Sutherland, and the principles of that philosophy remained the guiding stars of his approach to constitutional interpretation as a member of the Supreme Court. Sutherland served as United States Senator from Utah from 1905 to 1916, when he was defeated for reelection. He then established a law practice in Washington and was elected president of the American Bar Association. Sutherland was an early supporter of Warren G. Harding, and was regarded by some as Harding's "Colonel House" as a result of his prominent role in Harding's election to the presidency in 1920.

Sutherland had long been recognized as a potential Supreme Court Justice and had received serious consideration by President Taft for the vacancy finally filled by Van Devanter. Although Taft himself preceded Sutherland on the Court, replacing Chief Justice White in 1921, he wrote Sutherland that he "looked forward to having you on the bench with me. I know, as you do, that the President intends to put you there. . . . Our views are much alike, and it is important that they prevail." Sutherland's time finally came when Justice Clarke resigned on September 5, 1922. Harding immediately sent Sutherland's name to the Senate where it was confirmed the same day.

On the Court, Sutherland's best known opinion was his invalidation of the minimum wage for women on liberty of contract grounds in *Adkins* v. *Children's Hospital* (1923). He was soon recognized as a member of the solid conservative majority of Taft, Butler, McReynolds, Van Devanter, and Sanford that directed constitutional development in the United States during the 1920s. His opinion for the majority in the *Carter Coal Company* case (1936), with its emphasis on denying that either manufacturing or labor relations could be regulated under the Commerce Clause, seemed to validate the protests of employer groups against the NLRA and caused despair among those seeking an effective power to govern. Sutherland was not unaffected by the growing protest against the trend of the Court's decisions during the 1930s. "There is a more or less prevalent opinion abroad in the land," he wrote in January 1937, "that some judges are ruthless from pure depravity, and are indifferent to what others think about their decisions. There may be such, although I doubt it. At any rate, I am not one of them. I think almost every man prefers approval rather than disapproval of what he does." But a judge, Sutherland continued, must not allow what he does to be "influenced by his desire for approval or his fear of disapproval."

It is one of the ironies of the crisis of 1937 that both Justices Sutherland and Van Devanter would probably have retired before 1937 had not a chance event occurred in 1933. One of the early measures of the New Deal was the Economy Act of 1933, which reduced all federal salaries and pensions in the face of declining federal revenues. Justice Holmes had retired from the Court in 1932 under a statute permitting the Justices to retire at full pay after ten years of service on the Court.

The effect of the Economy Act, however, was to reduce Holmes' pension, with the result that there was hesitancy on the part of Justices Sutherland and Van Devanter to retire during the 1930s because of their distrust of Congress and their unhappiness over the treatment of Holmes. The result was that both Van Devanter and Sutherland remained on the Court in 1937, casting their votes generally against the New Deal.

The third member of the conservative bloc was Justice James Clark McReynolds. Born in Kentucky and educated at Vanderbilt University, McReynolds first achieved a degree of political prominence when he was appointed by President Taft to prosecute the Tobacco Trust, but he resigned when Taft's Attorney General, George Wickersham, authorized an agreement allowing the Tobacco Trust to retain its holdings. McReynolds' resignation under such circumstances made him something of a hero among those favoring strict enforcement of the antitrust laws. McReynolds was appointed Attorney General by Woodrow Wilson in 1913 and a year later Wilson appointed him to the Court.

Still a bachelor at seventy-five, McReynolds was probably the most disliked Justice both on and off the Court because of his thoroughly disagreeable temperament and his blatant prejudices. Even during the Wilson administration he had failed to cooperate with his colleagues and had alienated members of Congress. And on the Court, even Chief Justice Taft, who was always glad to have his vote in support of conservative constitutionalism, found McReynolds selfish, prejudiced, "and one who seems to delight in making others uncomfortable. . . . He has a continual grouch. . . ." Filing from the courtroom one day during the 1930s, Justice Stone remarked to McReynolds that the argument which they had just heard "was the dullest I ever heard in my life." "The only duller thing I can think of," McReynolds snapped, "is to hear you read one of your opinions." Because of his dislike of Jews,

McReynolds preferred to work at home rather than in his office, which was next to that of Brandeis, and when asked his opinion of Justice Cardozo soon after the latter's appointment in 1932, he replied, "He is just a Jew."

McReynolds was profoundly disturbed by the election of Franklin Roosevelt in 1932, and warned a friend privately that if the new President "surrounds himself with alien-minded men who have no real appreciation of our institutions or a lot whose ideas are out of accord with experience, he is lost. . . . It's no time for theorists who want to try out new plans of government. . . . Also he will fall into the ditch if he permits himself to be influenced by such men as the two Hebrews who are on the bench. The last one appointed, if possible, is more dangerous than the first." McReynolds must have felt that his fears of "alien-minded" advisers around the President were more than realized as the administration secured the passage of what to him were palpably unconstitutional measures, and when the administration's repudiation of the payment of contracts in gold was upheld by the Court in the *Gold Clause* cases (1935) ,* McReynolds could only mourn the passing of the Constitution. "The Constitution as many of us understood it," he said, "the instrument that has meant so much to us, is gone."

The final member of the conservative bloc was Justice Pierce Butler, a Minnesota Democrat at the time of his appointment to the Court. Butler had been a successful railroad attorney and had served on the Board of Regents of the University of Minnesota, a position he was said to have used to purge "radicals" from the faculty during the World War I period of hysteria. Strongly supported by Chief Justice Taft, Butler was appointed to the Court by Harding in 1923. As Taft neared death in 1929, he had written Butler that he feared for the preservation of conservative constitutionalism

* *Perry* v. *United States,* 294 U.S. 330 (1935) ; *Norman* v. *Baltimore & Ohio Ry. Co.,* 294 U.S. 240 (1935) .

and that they must hope for "continued life of enough of the present membership . . . to prevent disastrous reversals of our present attitude. With Van and Mac and Sutherland and you and Sanford, there will be five to steady the boat . . . we must not all give up at once."

Taft and Sanford had passed from the scene in 1930, but Van Devanter, Sutherland, Butler, and McReynolds were still "steadying the boat," maintaining the custom, begun by Taft, of meeting together often and with the aid of Justice Roberts controlling the decision of cases testing the most important policies of the New Deal. The conservative four were convinced, as they indicated in the *Carter* (1936), *Alton Railroad* (1935), and *Butler* (1936) cases, that the federal government's power under the Commerce Clause could not be extended to manufacturing, mining, and agricultural production and that the direct-indirect effects formula was fundamental to the preservation of state power and to the restriction of federal power within its proper limits. They had, in addition, composed four of the majority of five on the Court that had invalidated the minimum wage in the *Adkins* case (1923), and with the aid of Justice Roberts, continued its vitality by invalidating New York's minimum wage statute in *Morehead* v. *New York* (1936). The combination of their views on commerce and due process, separated from the context of constitutional doctrine, amounted essentially to a determination to preserve as much as possible of a laissez faire economic order. Having reached maturity during the period when the courts had begun to accept as their proper function the prevention of legislative abridgments of property rights as defined by classical economic theory, the "Four Horsemen" unhesitatingly accepted this as their duty and continued with substantial success in the 1930s to make their views those of the Supreme Court itself.

Ranged against the conservative bloc on the Court were Justices Brandeis, Stone, and Cardozo, with Louis Brandeis, at the age of eighty-one in 1937, the overshadowing symbol of liberalism in the law. Having received his legal education at Harvard Law School, where he compiled the most brilliant record ever recorded, Brandeis prospered sufficiently in his Boston law practice by the turn of the century to devote an increasing amount of his time to public affairs. Brandeis thus set out to become the "people's lawyer," representing what he believed to be the public interest in proceedings involving insurance companies, railroads, labor unions, and most other areas of business and industrial affairs. His most noted activity was his defense of labor laws that produced the famous "Brandeis brief" filed before the Supreme Court in Muller v. Oregon, 208 U.S. 412 (1908). To Brandeis, the overriding need in the law was the equipping of both lawyers and judges with sufficiently broad training to enable them to keep the law abreast of the rapid rate of technological change in the twentieth century. "The judge came to the bench unequipped with the necessary knowledge of economic and social science," he said, "and his judgment suffered likewise through lack of equipment in the lawyers who presented the cases to him. One can hardly escape the conclusion that a lawyer who has not studied economics and sociology is very apt to become a public enemy."

Brandeis had been a Republican since his law school days and had voted for Taft in 1908, but in 1912 he supported Woodrow Wilson after Theodore Roosevelt had supplanted Robert La Follette as the leading progressive Republican contender for the presidency. Wilson relied on Brandeis for advice on policy matters during the campaign, and Brandeis spoke on behalf of Wilson's candidacy in the East and Midwest. As a result, Brandeis was in active contention for the post of Attorney General in Wilson's cabinet, but James McReynolds was finally selected. Wilson, however, rewarded Brandeis for his support when he nominated him to succeed Joseph R. Lamar on the Supreme Court in January 1916.

The immediate uproar from business leaders and conservatives whom Brandeis had alienated in his service as "people's lawyer" was almost deafening. To William Howard Taft, Brandeis' nomination to the Court was one of the "deepest wounds that I have had as an American and a lover of the Constitution and a believer in progressive conservatism that a man such as Brandeis could be put in the Court. He is a muckraker, an emotionalist for his own purpose, a socialist . . . a man who has certain high ideals . . . of great tenacity of purpose and, in my judgment, of much power for evil. . . ." Seven past presidents of the American Bar Association, including Taft, pronounced Brandeis "not a fit person to be a member of the Supreme Court of the United States." Wilson, as was characteristic during his first term, held his party in the Senate with an iron grip, and Brandeis was confirmed by a vote of 47 to 22 on May 24, 1916.

In answer to a charge made during the fight over his confirmation in the Senate that he did not believe in a written Constitution, Brandeis had written the Attorney General that his "views in regard to the Constitution are as you know very much like those of Mr. Justice Holmes." This proved to be the case, and, despite basic philosophic differences between the two men, Holmes' and Brandeis' dissents became an increasingly persistent caveat to the dominant conservative constitutionalism of the Taft Court of the 1920s. The two dissenters were joined during the 1920s by a third, Harlan Fiske Stone.

Stone had received his law degree from Columbia University Law School in 1896, and in 1910 he returned to Columbia as Dean of the Law School. President Coolidge selected Stone as Attorney General to cleanse the Department of Justice following Harry Daugherty's scandal-ridden term in that post. When Justice McKenna resigned in 1925, Stone was appointed by Coolidge as McKenna's replacement on the Court. Stone readily admitted that although he had "taught and studied law for a great many years," he had come "only incidentally

. . . upon the field of constitutional law." There was, therefore, a period of incubation for Stone during the 1920s before his position on important constitutional questions was finally formulated. At first Stone was under the genial spell of Chief Justice Taft, but he broke completely from the conservative majority on the Court around 1927, and was soon aligning himself with Holmes and Brandeis in dissent. Taft was much chagrined by Stone's defection, and wondered "how experience as the head of a law school and supervising a law journal helps in making a first-class judge." By 1929 Taft had concluded that Stone, like Brandeis, Holmes, and Herbert Hoover, was a "progressive."

By the time of the New Deal, Stone had been fully won over to the preachments of Brandeis and Holmes on the use of the Court's power, and it was he who phrased the liberal's philosophy of judicial self-restraint in its classic form in his dissent in the *Butler* case (1936). The majority opinion by Justice Roberts had declared the Agricultural Adjustment Act's use of the spending power to regulate farm production invalid as an invasion of the reserved powers of the states. While admitting that the exercise of the power to tax and spend by Congress was not limited by the specific grants of power in the Constitution, the majority held that if such an act were sustained Congress would "become a parliament of the whole people subject to no restrictions save such as are self-imposed." Stone exploded in a dissent so vehement that Roberts complained to Chief Justice Hughes. Even after some softening, the dissent was a scathing indictment of the majority opinion of the Court. Stone admitted that the power to tax and spend might be abused, but so might judicial power.

> A tortured construction of the Constitution is not to be justified, by recourse to extreme examples of reckless congressional spending which might occur if courts could not prevent it. . . . Such suppositions are addressed to the mind accustomed to believe that it is the business of the courts to sit in judgment on the wisdom of

legislative action. Courts are not the only agency of government that must be assumed to have capacity to govern. Congress and the courts both unhappily may falter or be mistaken in the performance of their constitutional duty. But interpretation of our great charter of government which proceeds on any assumption that the responsibility for the preservation of our institutions is the exclusive concern of any one of the three branches of government, or that it alone can save them from destruction, is far more likely, in the long run, "to obliterate the constituent members" of "an indestructible union of indestructible states" than the frank recognition that language, even of a constitution, may mean what it says. . . .

Stone's dissent in the *Butler* case (1936), in which he was joined by Justices Brandeis and Cardozo, in addition to being a classic argument for judicial self-restraint was a source of encouragement to New Dealers who sought broader constitutional power as an instrument of reform. As Edward S. Corwin noted, for the first time members of the Court had indicated that the use of federal power by the New Deal was not entirely untenable under the Constitution. Stone also was the spokesman for the liberal bloc in its dissent from the majority's opinion in the *Morehead* case (1936) in which New York's minimum wage statute was invalidated on liberty of contract grounds. "There is grim irony," Stone said, "in speaking of the freedom of contract of those whom because of their economic necessities give their services for less than is needful to keep body and soul together." He said that time had proved the inadequacy of the rule of the *Adkins* case (1923) as a doctrine of constitutional law. Since it was decided, Stone declared:

> . . . we have had opportunity to learn that a wage is not always the resultant of free bargaining between employers and employees; that it may be one forced upon employees by their economic necessities and upon employers by the most ruthless of their competitors. We have had opportunity to perceive more clearly that a wage insufficient to support the worker does not visit its consequences upon him alone; that it may affect profoundly the

entire economic structure of society and, in any case, that it casts upon every tax payer, and on government itself, the burden of solving problems of poverty, subsistence, health, and morals of large numbers in the community. Because of their nature and extent they are public problems. A generation ago they were for the individual to solve; today they are the burden of the nation.

The *Morehead* and *Carter Coal Company* decisions (1936) were very discouraging to Stone. "We finished the term of Court yesterday," he wrote privately in 1936. "I think in many ways one of the most disastrous in its history. At any rate it seems to me that the Court has been needlessly narrow and obscurantic in its outlook." The Court, it seemed to Stone, had "tied Uncle Sam up in a hard knot." The third member of the liberal bloc, Justice Benjamin N. Cardozo, agreed with Stone's estimate of the Court's performance in 1936. "We did indeed have a hard year in the court," he wrote Stone. "Next year may be bad, but certainly can't be worse. . . ."

Cardozo, the son of Portuguese-Jewish parents, came to the Court after establishing a brilliant record as both a judge and a scholar of the law on the New York Court of Appeals. When Justice Holmes announced his retirement from the Court in January 1932 Cardozo's reputation made him the only logical successor. President Hoover, under pressure from leaders of the bar and the Senate, soon announced the appointment of the New York Democrat to the Court. Justice Stone felt so strongly about the appropriateness of Cardozo's appointment to the Court that he told Hoover, his good friend, that he would resign from the Court if necessary to remove the possible political liability of having three New Yorkers on the Court.

Stone had predicted that Cardozo would "look upon the controversial questions which come before our Court as I do . . . ," and this proved to be the case as Cardozo quickly joined Brandeis and Stone on the liberal wing of the Court.

In 1924 Cardozo had written that in judging it was "vain to seek a sovereign talisman; that the treasure box does not spring open at the magic of a whispered word; that there is no one method of judging, supreme over its competitors, but only a choice of methods changing with the problem." And it was in this spirit that he attacked the Court majority's rigid use of the direct-indirect effects formula in deciding the extent of Congress' power under the Commerce Clause. While concurring in the Court's opinion in the *Schechter* case (1935), Cardozo did not accept Chief Justice Hughes' use of the direct-indirect effects formula, but emphasized that upon the facts of the case, the NIRA's regulation of wages and hours in the live poultry industry could not stand as a valid regulation of commerce. In the *Carter* case (1936), however, Cardozo dissented from the majority's use of the direct-indirect effects formula to classify manufacturing and mining enterprises as "local" in nature and argued that upon the facts of the case the Bituminous Coal Act could be upheld as a valid regulation enacted under the Commerce Clause. Cardozo said:

> Mining and agriculture and manufacture are not interstate commerce considered by themselves, yet their relation to that commerce may be such that for the protection of one there is need to regulate the other. . . . Sometimes it is said that the relation must be "direct" to bring that power into play. In many circumstances such a description will be sufficiently precise to meet the needs of the occasion. But a great principle of constitutional law is not susceptible of comprehensive statement in an adjective.

In each case, Cardozo argued, instead of rigidly applying the direct-indirect effects formula, the Court should consider whether or not the facts justified congressional regulation of "local" activities in order to effectively regulate commerce. The relation between "'local" activities and commerce:

> . . . may be tenuous or the opposite according to the facts. Always the setting of the facts is to be viewed if one would know the closeness of the tie. Perhaps, if one group of adjectives is to

be chosen in preference to another, "intimate" and "remote" will be found to be as good as any. At all events, "direct" and "indirect," even if accepted as sufficient, must not be read too narrowly.

The Justice who aligned himself with the conservative four and thereby permitted the commerce and liberty of contract decisions that Cardozo, Stone, and Brandeis attacked was Owen J. Roberts. Roberts had been born in the Germantown section of Philadelphia in May 1875. He concentrated on the study of Greek as an undergraduate at the University of Pennsylvania and after receiving his degree in 1891 he considered for a time becoming a teacher of Greek. Instead he entered the University of Pennsylvania Law School where he received his law degree in 1898 with highest honors. In 1924 Roberts was appointed by President Coolidge to prosecute the Teapot Dome scandal. He was occupied with this involved litigation for six years and had become nationally known in that assignment when the Senate rejected President Hoover's nomination of Judge John J. Parker to the Court in 1930. Hoover then turned to Roberts, a life long Republican, and the Senate quickly confirmed Roberts' appointment to the Court.

"He is a hard worker, has a good mind, and has had a wide range of experience," Justice Stone wrote in appraisal of Roberts. "I should expect him to deal in the liberal way with important constitutional problems, because he has the type of mind that would take in all aspects of the problem." The new Justice seemed to be bearing out Stone's prediction during 1934 when he joined the Chief Justice, Stone, Brandeis, and Cardozo to sustain a Minnesota statute conferring on the courts the power to postpone mortgage foreclosures,* and in *Nebbia* v. *New York*,† he voted to sustain a New York statute fixing the price of milk against a challenge that it interfered with liberty and property rights guaranteed by the Due Proc-

---

* Home Building & Loan Association v. Blaisdell, 290 U.S. 398 (1934).
† 291 U.S. 502 (1934).

ess Clause of the Fourteenth Amendment. Roberts' uncertainty began to tell when the *Nebbia* case was under consideration by the Court. He paced the floor of his Washington home most of the night before deciding how to cast his vote. Finally in 1935 Roberts swung to the conservative side and wrote the majority opinion in the *Alton Railroad* case, holding the Railroad Retirement Act invalid under the Commerce Clause and the Due Process Clause of the Fifth Amendment.

During 1936 Roberts was again on the side of the conservatives, along with the Chief Justice, in the *Butler* case. Writing the opinion invalidating the AAA Roberts asserted the concept that the Court was not making policy in deciding constitutional cases.

> It is sometimes said that the court assumes a power to overrule or control the action of the people's representatives. This is a misconception. The Constitution is the supreme law of the land ordained and established by the people. All legislation must conform to the principles it lays down. When an act of Congress is appropriately challenged in the courts as not conforming to the constitutional mandate the judicial branch of the government has only one duty,—to lay the article of the Constitution which is invoked beside the statute which is challenged and to decide whether the latter squares with the former. All the court does, or can do, is to announce its considered judgment upon the question. The only power it has, if such it may be called, is the power of judgment. The court neither approves nor condemns any legislative policy.

Roberts also joined with the majority in the *Carter* and *Morehead* cases (1936) that denied the power to regulate wages to both the federal and state governments and thus created a "no-man's-land" in which neither level of government could act. In a memorandum published after his death Roberts explained that he joined the majority in the *Morehead* case only because the New York minimum wage statute involved in the case could not be distinguished from the statute invalidated in the *Adkins* case (1923). The counsel for New

York had not asked the Court to overrule the *Adkins* case, but instead had argued that the New York act was distinguishable from the act involved in the *Adkins* case. Roberts thought this argument was "disingenuous and born of timidity" and voted with the conservatives to invalidate the New York statute. Due to Stone's rigorous attack on the majority's position, Justice Butler, who had been assigned the task of writing the majority opinion, added material to his opinion which made the decision rest upon a reaffirmation of the *Adkins* case rather than on the narrow basis to which Roberts had agreed. "My proper course," Roberts said later, "would have been to concur specially on the narrow ground I had taken. I did not do so. But at the conference in the Court I said that I did not propose to review and re-examine the *Adkins* case until a case would come to the Court requiring that this should be done."

To the country at large, however, it appeared that a majority of five on the Court still believed that the doctrine of liberty of contract prohibited state regulation of minimum wages, and at the Republican convention in 1936 a platform plank was adopted repudiating the decision and advocating the enactment of minimum wage laws without a constitutional amendment. Stone, noting the action of the Republican convention and other expressions of disapproval of the *Morehead* decision (1936), wrote Brandeis that it "seems to be dawning on a good many minds that after all there may be something in the protest of the so-called liberal minority." "Yes," Brandeis replied, "the consternation of the enemy is encouraging."

The equivocal role of Roberts in the *Morehead* case (1936) was matched, however, by the behavior of Chief Justice Hughes in the period prior to Roosevelt's attack on the Court. Hughes' career had been one of remarkable success. He had been successively a leading member of the bar, a much publicized investigator of corruption in New York in 1905, reform Governor of New York from 1906 to 1910, an Associate Justice of the Supreme Court from 1910 to 1916, unsuccessful Republican candidate for President in 1916, Secretary of State under Harding and Coolidge, World Court Judge from 1928 to 1930, and finally, he had been appointed Chief Justice by Hoover in 1930. Thus as a public figure, Hughes overshadowed his colleagues on the Court and as such was the central political figure on the Court in the constitutional crisis of 1937.

As an Associate Justice Hughes had demonstrated a liberal inclination on constitutional issues. He wrote the Court's opinion in the famous *Shreveport* case (1914) that extended the federal commerce power to include the regulation of rates charged by an interstate railroad for operations totally within one state. Hughes had also dissented, along with Justices Holmes and Day, in *Coppage* v. *Kansas* (1915), where a majority of the Court had invalidated a statute outlawing the yellow-dog contract. Hughes' record as Chief Justice, however, was rather equivocal in several cases. He wrote the unanimous opinion of the Court in the *Texas & New Orleans Railroad* case (1930) sustaining the Railway Labor Act of 1926 and creating a precedent for the broader use of the commerce power, but in the *Schechter* case (1936), he argued that the distinction "between direct and indirect effects of intrastate transactions upon interstate commerce must be recognized as a fundamental one, essential to the maintenance of our constitutional system." In the *Alton Railroad* case (1935), however, he joined Stone, Brandeis, and Cardozo in dissenting from the majority's denial that a railroad pension plan was a valid exercise of congressional power under the Commerce Clause. But the Chief Justice again joined Roberts and the conservatives in the *Butler* case (1936). In the *Morehead* case (1936) he dissented only on the narrow ground that the New York minimum wage statute could be distinguished from the statute involved in the *Adkins* case (1923).

In the *Carter Coal Company* case (1936), Hughes concurred with the majority's view that mining and manufacturing enterprises, and the employee-employer relations incidental to such enterprises, could not be regulated under the Commerce Clause, dissenting only on the grounds that the price fixing provisions of the Bituminous Coal Act were valid and separable from the labor provisions. He agreed, he wrote, that "production—in this case mining—which precedes commerce, is not itself commerce; and that the power to regulate commerce among the several States is not a power to regulate industry within a state." Congress could not use its protective authority under the Commerce Clause, he continued:

> . . . as a pretext for the exertion of power to regulate activities and relations within the States which affect interstate commerce only indirectly. Otherwise, in view of the multitude of indirect effects, Congress in its discretion could assume control of virtually all the activities of the people to the subversion of the fundamental principle of the Constitution. If the people desire to give Congress the power to regulate industries within the States, and the relations of employers and employees in those industries, they are at liberty to declare their will in the appropriate manner, but it is not for the Court to amend the Constitution by judicial decision.

Hughes thus seemed to be arguing that the "fundamental" distinction between direct and indirect effects on interstate commerce consigned the effects of labor relations in production industries to the category of "indirect effects," and that such relations could therefore not be regulated by Congress unless the people were to adopt a constitutional amendment conferring such power on Congress. The Chief Justice's position in several important cases, and particularly in the *Carter* case (1936), must have therefore contributed to the impression in both the administration and the country at large that the Court would remain adamant in denying Congress and the President the power to govern. Robert Jackson reflected the reaction of New Dealers to the Court in saying that the Court seemed to have not only "challenged the policies of the New Deal but erected judicial barriers to the reasonable exercise of legislative powers, both state and national, to meet the urgent needs of a twentieth-century community."

THE COURT-PACKING PLAN

With the court-packing plan, President Roosevelt hoped to remove these barriers to the exercise of governmental power. Roosevelt had considered the possibility of a constitutional amendment that would have broadened congressional power to deal with social and economic problems. This possibility had been rejected because Roosevelt estimated that the chances were about even of obtaining the two-thirds majority in both houses of Congress necessary for the proposal of constitutional amendments, and that the process of ratification by state legislatures would have been slow, perhaps delaying ratification until 1940 or 1941. Roosevelt also felt that the conservative opposition to the New Deal would mount an effective campaign against the ratification of such an amendment. "If I were in private practice and without a conscience," Roosevelt wrote Felix Frankfurter, "I would gladly undertake for a drawing account of fifteen or twenty million dollars (easy enough to raise) to guarantee that an amendment would not be ratified prior to the 1940 elections. In other words, I think I could withhold ratification in thirteen states and I think you will agree with my judgment on this." Roosevelt thus rejected the idea of a constitutional amendment to overcome the barriers to the New Deal erected by the Court's decisions despite the fact that he had assured the platform committee of the 1936 Democratic national convention that if New Deal measures proved to be unconstitutional a "clarifying amendment" to the Constitution would be sought by the administration.

Roosevelt consulted few members of his administration in regard to the court-packing plan, relying principally upon Attorney General Homer Cummings and Solicitor General Stanley Reed to draft the measure, and he did not consult the congressional leadership prior to his announcement of the plan. The usually adroit Roosevelt also badly bungled the introduction of the court-packing plan by using ingenuous arguments on its behalf. The plan was necessary, he argued, because the Court was behind in its work, the implication being that this condition was due to the old age and inefficiency of the Justices. Yet the oldest member of the Court was Justice Brandeis, regarded as friendly to the New Deal, and in fact the Court had been current with its docket since shortly after the Judiciary Act of 1925 was enacted.* The court-packing plan never really overcame the initial handicap created by the use of these basically dishonest arguments in its favor.

"Nobody knows what you are getting at and nobody knows what your grievance is," Assistant Attorney General Robert Jackson told the President. "You sound off about old age, and here Brandeis is [our] best friend on the Supreme Court. This thing has got to be put in different terms or you're going to lose the country." As a result of such advice, Roosevelt ultimately abandoned the initial arguments offered in support of court-packing and argued instead that his proposal was necessary because the Court was blocking badly needed reforms overwhelmingly approved by the people in 1932, 1934, and 1936. Presenting the case for the plan before the Senate Judiciary Committee, Assistant Attorney General Jackson also argued that the "whole program approved by the people in 1932, 1934, and 1936 is in danger of being lost in a maze of constitutional metaphors. . . . That the conflict between the Court and the elective branches of the Government is entering a new phase is apparent from the extensive assertion of the right to disregard acts of Congress, which is subtly transferring the process of judicial review into a veto power over legisla-

* The Judiciary Act of 1925 greatly expanded the discretionary power of the Court to determine which of the cases appealed to it should be heard. After 1925, therefore, the Court could substantially control its workload and had been generally abreast of the cases on its docket.

tion." The Court itself undoubtedly had no desire to exercise such a veto power, Jackson continued, but "powerful interests, by carrying all causes lost in Congress to the Supreme Court, and by resisting lawful authority, meanwhile, are forcing that consequence upon the Court with its effective, if unconscious, consent."

Despite this shifting of the administration's arguments for the court-packing plan, it is now clear that Roosevelt overestimated the extent to which public opinion and the Congress would support him in such a proposal. While indicating some fluctuations during the court-packing fight, the Gallup Poll never indicated that a majority of the public supported the plan. Because the Senate was regarded as the most pro-New Deal of the houses of Congress, the administration wanted to secure Senate passage of the plan first, hoping the momentum this generated behind the plan would also carry it to victory in the House. The Senate, however, split into roughly three equal groups, composed of those opposing the plan, those favorable, and those who were undecided. Instead of quick approval by the Senate Judiciary Committee and passage by the Senate itself, the court-packing plan was thus subjected to extended hearings and months of delay in committee.

Their ranks decimated by the overwhelming Democratic victory in 1936, the Republicans in the Congress shrewdly decided to avoid strong, public opposition to the court-packing plan in the belief that defeat of the plan would be more likely if the opposition to it was led by Democrats and that Republican opposition would only tend to unite the Democrats behind the plan. This strategy paid off handsomely, since Senator Burton K. Wheeler, a long-time progressive Democrat from Montana, assumed the leadership of the Senate opposition to the plan with the result that the court-packing fight became largely an intra-Democratic Party fight. Wheeler sought some device by which to throw the prestige of the Supreme Court against the plan, and with this in mind contacted Justice Brandeis. Brandeis immediately suggested that Wheeler contact Chief Justice Hughes, whom Wheeler found willing to appear personally before the Senate Judiciary Committee in regard to the plan. This idea, however, was vetoed by Brandeis, but a letter from the Chief Justice to the Judiciary Committee commenting on the court-packing plan was finally agreed on.

In his letter to the Judiciary Committee, which Senator Wheeler presented with much fanfare on March 22, Hughes ignored the administration's shift from its initial arguments in favor of court-packing to the later, and more defensible, argument that the plan was justified because the Court was blocking programs overwhelmingly supported by the public. Instead, Hughes attacked the initial arguments offered in support of the plan, hitting the administration at its weakest point. "There is no congestion of cases upon our calendar," Hughes said. "This gratifying condition has obtained for several years." The addition of more Justices to the Court, Hughes continued, "apart from any question of policy, which I do not discuss, would not promote the efficiency of the Court. It is believed that it would impair that efficiency so long as the Court acts as a unit. There would be more judges to hear, more judges to confer, more judges to discuss, more judges to be convinced and to decide. The present number of justices is thought to be large enough so far as the prompt, adequate, and efficient conduct of the work of the Court is concerned." With additional Justices on the Court, it had been suggested that the Justices could sit in panels and dispose of more cases. The Chief Justice, however, pointed out that the "constitution does not appear to authorize two or more Supreme Courts or two or more parts of a supreme court functioning in effect as separate courts."

Hughes stated in his letter that "on account of shortness of time" he had been unable to consult all members of the Court but that he was "confident it is in accord with the views of the

Justices. . . . I should say, however," the Chief Justice closed, "that I have been able to consult with Mr. Justice Van Devanter and Mr. Justice Brandeis, and I am at liberty to say that the statement is approved by them." The fact that representatives of the liberal and conservative blocs on the Court concurred in the letter of course gave added weight to its contents, but it is now apparent that at least two members of the Court, Justices Stone and Cardozo, would not have accepted all of the views expressed in the letter. It was also misleading for the Chief Justice to plead lack of time in which to consult with the remaining Justices, since all of them were in Washington at the time and could have easily been reached. Hughes was undoubtedly aware that if the Justices could not agree upon major issues before the Court, they were unlikely to be unanimous on the contents of his letter, and a lack of unanimity would have detracted from the usefulness of the letter in the public debate over the court-packing plan. The impression that the public was given from Hughes' remarks was that the Court was unanimous in supporting the views expressed in the letter, an impression encouraged by Senator Wheeler when he stated that it "should be borne in mind that, although the members of the Supreme Court may have differed on a great many things, they are unanimous with reference to the letter of the Chief Justice; at least that is my understanding of the matter."

Secretary of Interior Harold Ickes recognized quite clearly the adroitness of Hughes' tactics in his letter to the Judiciary Committee. "It was good tactics," Ickes said. ". . . the President's special message . . . was almost entirely based on the proposition that we needed more federal judges because, on account of old age and decrepitude, we haven't enough able-bodied judges to keep up with the work of the courts. We abandoned this ground some time ago, but, shrewdly, Hughes chose to fight his skirmish where we were the weakest. . . . Although the letter carefully negatived any suggestion that the

Court was discussing the broad, general policy involved, the whole thing has the appearance of a unanimous Supreme Court opposing the President's proposal." Felix Frankfurter, writing to Roosevelt privately, denounced Hughes' tactics before the Judiciary Committee. *"That,"* Frankfurter said, "was a characteristic Hughes performance—part and parcel of that pretended withdrawal from considerations of policy, while trying to shape them, which is the core of the mischief of which the majority have been so long guilty. That Brandeis should have been persuaded to allow the Chief to use his name is a source of sadness to me that I need hardly dwell on to you."

THE SIT-DOWN STRIKES

In addition to the court-packing crisis in 1937, the country was also faced with a crisis of the first magnitude in industry. In the face of adamant refusals by employers to recognize the right of workers to organize and bargain collectively, the workers began to occupy industrial plants and businesses in sit-down strikes across the country. From September 1936 to May 1937, 484,711 workers engaged in sit-downs that closed plants employing over one million workers. The peak came in March 1937 when 192,642 workers sat down in their plants, the most spectacular strike being by the CIO United Automobile Workers against General Motors at Flint, Michigan. John L. Lewis publicly pointed out to President Roosevelt that for "six months during the Presidential campaign the economic royalists represented by General Motors and the Du Ponts contributed their money and used their energy to drive this Administration from power. The Administration asked labor for help to repel this attack and labor gave it. The same economic royalists now have their fangs in labor. The workers of this country," Lewis warned, "expect this Administration to help the strikers in every reasonable way." The striking workers in Flint sent out word that any attempt to dislodge them from the plants would result in a "bloody massacre of the workers." Governor Frank Murphy of Michigan refused to use the militia to drive the workers out of the automobile plants fearing bloody violence and ultimately General Motors officials met with the union leaders and finally agreed to recognize the union. The success of the General Motors sit-down strike encouraged the use of this tactic in other industries.

As the sit-down strikes reached their peak in the spring of 1937, the *Jones & Laughlin* case and the other cases testing the validity of the National Labor Relations Act came before the Supreme Court for oral argument. The use of such tactics by workers to gain recognition of their right to organize and bargain collectively, tactics regarded by many as revolutionary, must have underscored the significance of the *Jones & Laughlin* case to the members of the Court. The Court thus faced dual crises in the spring of 1937—an industrial crisis arising out of issues that were directly before the Court in the cases testing the validity of the NLRA, and a constitutional crisis brought on by the court-packing proposal. How the Court decided the *Jones & Laughlin* case and the other NLRA cases would determine to a great extent how both crises facing the Court and the country would ultimately be resolved.

⊸§ 6 §⊷

THE NLRA BEFORE
THE COURT

⊷———————◆———————⊶

On February 9, 1937, four days after President Roosevelt submitted his court-packing plan to Congress, the Supreme Court
began to hear arguments in the *Jones & Laughlin* case and in
its four companion cases testing the constitutionality of the
National Labor Relations Act.   The principal arguments
both for and against the validity of the act were fully can-
vassed in the *Jones & Laughlin* and *Associated Press* cases.*

---

* In addition to the primary parties in these five cases, there were
amicus curiae briefs filed by the American Newspaper Publishers Association and the American Newspaper Guild in the *Associated Press* case,
an American Federation of Labor *amicus curiae* brief in the *Fruehauf*
case, and *amicus* briefs filed on behalf of the Amalgamated Association of
Street, Electric Railway and Motor Coach Employees Union and the
Pennsylvania Greyhound Lines in the *Washington, Virginia and Maryland
Coach Company* case.

COMMERCE CLAUSE ARGUMENTS:
BUSINESS' CASE

In the *Associated Press* case the NLRB felt it possessed a case that tested the application of the NLRA to an enterprise clearly interstate in nature. However, John W. Davis in his brief and in oral argument before the Court argued on behalf of the Associated Press that Morris Watson's duties in the New York AP office had not been interstate in nature. Editorial employees, such as Watson, Davis argued, were not engaged in the interstate transmission of news but rather in the formulation and rewriting of news *prior* to its transmission in interstate commerce. Such employees, Davis said, were thus analogous "to employees in a manufacturing plant engaged in transforming the raw materials into the completed article." And a strike by such employees would have the same effect upon commerce as a strike by production employees in any production industry—an indirect effect, and the Court had held in cases from the Sugar Trust case (1895) to the *Carter Coal Company* case (1936) that indirect effects on commerce could not be reached by Congress under the Commerce Clause.

The government's argument that denial of the employees' right to organize by employers tended to cause labor disputes which in turn had the tendency to interrupt, burden, or obstruct interstate commerce, was denounced by Davis as a chain of speculation unsuitable as a basis of sound constitutional interpretation. "It is direct causes operating directly upon interstate commerce," Davis said, "with which Congress is empowered to deal." Masterful as always during oral argument, Davis declared on this point:

> The Associated Press is engaged in the dissemination of news. The dissemination of news constitutes interstate commerce. News cannot be disseminated unless it is gathered. News after it is

gathered cannot be used until it has been written. Editorial writers are necessary both to edit and to gather the news, and if no news is gathered no news can be transmitted. Editorial writers, being like most artists, perhaps temperamental, must be content, of a contented mind, before they can efficiently perform their duties. A contented mind can only be based upon satisfactory working conditions, hours, and terms of payment. Satisfactory working conditions, hours, and terms of payment can only be brought about by collective bargaining.

Ergo, to force the Associated Press to engage in collective bargaining is a bona-fide regulation of commerce. And that, I respectfully submit, is nothing but a repetition in argumentative form of a nursery rhyme of The House that Jack Built. You can stretch out the relation of cause and effect, according to the philosophers, to the very beginning of time, for I understand their theory is that there has been no interruption of cause and effect since the water first rolled back from the land, and probably beyond that we get to the cause. But [that is] not the revolution by which the Constitution of the United States can be interpreted or by which Congress can broaden its power to subjects that were never committed to it.

Finally, Davis contended that the provisions of the NLRA, taken as a whole, evidenced an intention on the part of Congress to subject the labor relations of all industries in the country to regulation by the NLRB. And this, after such decisions as those in the *Schechter* (1935) and *Carter* (1936) cases, was clearly beyond congressional power under the Commerce Clause. "That the regulation of the employer-employee relationship in all industry is not in any sense a regulation of interstate or foreign commerce," Davis said, "should require little if any elaboration. There appear to be few propositions in the realm of Constitutional law which are more fundamental or more clearly settled." And during oral argument Davis declared:

What is involved here, is the power of the Federal Government to make collective bargaining compulsory in all the industries of this country. We challenge that power. . . . If this law is a law at all, it must apply to the great and the small alike, and if this theory of interstate commerce can support this sort of intrusion, then it must be clear that no workman in the United States in any of its production industries can be discharged, or even the terms of his daily labor altered, and the place, without a hearing by the National Labor Board; and the very magnitude of the probable task ought to be enough to make men of average humility shrink from its assumption. [The reasoning] of the *Carter* and *Schechter* cases, dooms this statute beyond all reasonable hope of recovery.

Arguing on behalf of the Jones & Laughlin Steel Corporation, Earl F. Reed had a much easier task than John W. Davis in demonstrating that under the Court's prior decisions the NLRA was beyond Congress' power under the Commerce Clause. The doctrine of dual federalism by which the Court had held production to be an activity essentially reserved to the states under the Tenth Amendment, and the direct-indirect effects formula by which the Court had held that production only had an indirect effect on commerce as recently as in the *Carter* case (1936), appeared to make the NLRA invalid as applied to Jones & Laughlin. Reed thus argued in his brief that "the decisive factor" in the *Jones & Laughlin* case was that the discharged employees *"were unquestionably engaged in aiding the respondent's manufacturing activities in the Aliquippa works."*

Despite the government's attempts to confuse the issues, Reed said:

> . . . the Constitution requires the separation of State and Federal power. The decision of this Court, in [the *Schechter* case], is a mandate that the literal requirements of the Constitution must not be ignored. It may be true that purely internal affairs do indirectly affect interstate commerce, just as interstate commerce bears indirectly upon internal affairs, but while this might be urged as a reason for altering our Constitutional form of government, it is not an excuse for attempting to obliterate the Constitutional distinction between commerce and that which is not.

Earl Reed admitted that raw materials such as coal, limestone, and iron ore were shipped to Jones & Laughlin's Aliquippa plant in interstate commerce, but once they arrived at the plant, he argued, interstate commerce had ceased and did not begin again until the steel that was the product of the utilization and conversion of these raw materials was shipped to interstate markets. What occurred at the Aliquippa plant, Reed thus contended, was not interstate commerce but rather manufacturing or production, an activity clearly beyond the power of Congress to control under the Commerce Clause. And since the employees whose firing by Jones & Laughlin was alleged to violate the NLRA were employed in the manufacturing process at the Aliquippa plant, the application of the act in the *Jones & Laughlin* case was patently invalid under the Commerce Clause. The government's argument in the *Jones & Laughlin* case, Reed contended:

> . . . implicitly admits the remoteness of the connection between the discharge of [the] employees and the movement of interstate commerce, but seeks to justify the application of the statute because of the size and importance of the respondent's operations. So far as the effect on interstate commerce is concerned, there is in reality, no difference between the respondent's Aliquippa Plant and a neighborhood grocery store; the cause and effect may be larger, but the causal connection is just as remote.

The government relied heavily on the *Texas & New Orleans Railroad* case (1930) and the stream of commerce cases to support the validity of the NLRA under the Commerce Clause. Reed sought to distinguish the operations at the Jones & Laughlin plant from the activities that the Court had held Congress could validly regulate in those cases. The *Texas & New Orleans Railroad* case, he said, involved congressional regulation of an admittedly interstate industry, the railroads, while the NLRA as applied to Jones & Laughlin was an attempt to regulate a manufacturing industry, the activities of which were clearly local or intrastate in nature. In the stream of commerce cases the Court had upheld regulation of activities closely related to interstate movement or activities that directly affected or obstructed such movement, whereas in the manufacturing of steel from coal, limestone, and iron ore the interstate movement of these raw materials ended before the manufacturing process began, and the interstate movement did not begin again until the finished steel products were shipped in interstate commerce after their manufacture had occurred. Activities related to the manufacturing process did not occur in the stream of commerce nor did they affect commerce directly. Citing especially the *Carter* case (1936), Reed thus fully expected that the Court "will confine the doctrine of the grain exchange and stockyards cases to transactions which are intimately connected with the movement of commerce, or directly obstruct or impede it; and that it will not justify, as a regulation of commerce, a statute which *piles speculation upon speculation to attain its ends.*" On this point, he declared during oral argument:

> The Government argues that it is the stream of commerce. I shall not go into that except to point out this, that in *Stafford* v. *Wallace* and in *Board of Trade* v. *Olsen* the evidence and the matters before Congress showed beyond any doubt that these were select focal points in which practically all of the commerce passed. This mill is not in any way stationed in the stream of commerce. This plant into which we take coal and coke and limestone and turn out steel, is not any mere temporary stoppage in a stream of commerce coming from the West to the East. It is not comparable, and because Congress could regulate stockyards, it is a far cry to say that they could regulate the labor relations of an industry like the steel industry.

The NLRB had added to the record in the *Jones & Laughlin* case extensive testimony from labor relations experts and students of labor history implying that one of the leading causes of labor disputes which historically had had drastic effects on interstate commerce was the employers' denial of the right of their employees to organize into unions and bargain collectively. In regard to this testimony, Reed declared that it was "a defiance of reason and good judgment to argue that guesswork evidence of this character can bridge the distance between the discharge of . . . employees and the movement of interstate commerce." Hitting at this "Brandeis brief" tactic of the Board during oral argument, Reed said:

> Then, the record abounds with a mass of hypothetical testimony, hundreds of pages of it. After this hearing in Pittsburgh . . . they held hearings in Washington here for days, in which various persons came forward and gave a great deal of hypothetical testimony—labor persons who said they believe that organized labor and national unions were a good thing for labor. The Board took judicial notice of theses written by professors in colleges about the advantages of union labor, of declarations made years ago . . . and all it amounted to was a vast mass of opinion evidence that national unions would be a good thing for workers.
>
> And it was not confined to the steel industry. They went into the producing industries. They offered college theses. They offered public records. They even offered The Steel Dictator, a book written by Harvey O'Connor, as evidence to show that the stoppage of business and commerce was in large part due to strikes.
>
> It was on the basis of that testimony that the Board found that a labor dispute in the steel industry would interrupt commerce. This company was not shut down in 1919 when the labor strife occurred. It operated throughout. It has had no labor disturbance since 1892, but all these other intervening labor disturbances were used to show that they had a tendency to interrupt commerce.

In concluding his commerce argument Reed declared that for more "than a century this Court has steadfastly adhered to the simple, literal meaning which the great Marshall found in the commerce clause," while at the same time giving "assurance to the States, to their citizens and to the federal union that their respective rights and powers, as the Constitution fixes them, shall be preserved. . . ." The government, Reed said, was asking that "the traditions and precedents of a century be cast aside and the Constitution corrupted for the sake of a temporary expediency. To change *the established mean-*

ing of the Constitution now, by judicial decree, without a proper mandate from the people, would make a mockery of constitutional government."

COMMERCE CLAUSE ARGUMENTS:
THE GOVERNMENT'S CASE

Few attorneys have faced greater constitutional difficulties than the government attorneys who sought to persuade the Court of the NLRA's validity under the Constitution. The government's arguments on behalf of the NLRA were presented orally before the Court by Solicitor General Stanley Reed, Special Assistant Attorney General Charles Wyzanski, Jr., Chairman J. Warren Madden of the NLRB, and Charles Fahy, General Counsel of the Board.

Meeting the contentions of John W. Davis and Earl Reed that the NLRA was beyond the power of Congress to enact under the Commerce Clause, the government attorneys first challenged the contention, especially pressed by Davis, that the act was invalid because it was intended to apply to "all industry," and all industry obviously could not be regulated by Congress under the Commerce Clause. The government attorneys replied that the provisions in the act were clearly limited in their application to "interstate commerce" and to businesses in which labor disputes would "affect" interstate commerce, terms which the Court itself had used in describing the scope of congressional power under the Commerce Clause. Congress, they said, clearly intended that the NLRA should apply only to those businesses that it could validly reach under the commerce power. Secondly, the government argued, the act provided that the NLRB would initially decide whether the act applied to a particular business or industry, and that a Board decision was reviewable by the courts. If the Board applied the NLRA to businesses beyond the scope of the commerce power, the courts could review its determinations and reverse such Board decisions on a case by case basis. "Should the Board err in its application of the Act," the government counsel said, "the courts will correct the error by holding that the order exceeded the Act, not that the Act exceeded the commerce power."

In each of the cases testing the validity of the NLRA before the Court the government argued that the question in each case was whether or not the act had been validly applied to the particular business involved. In the *Associated Press* case the government's burden of demonstrating the interstate nature of the AP's operations was much lighter than its burden in the *Jones & Laughlin* case. Under Court decisions running back into the nineteenth century, it had been established that the communication of information across state lines was interstate commerce. The Court had thus held that Congress could regulate the interstate communication of messages via telegraph, and in the twentieth century this principle had been the basis of federal regulation of the new radio broadcasting industry. The Associated Press, the government pointed out, was involved in extensive communication of news via "leased wires" involving both interstate and foreign communication by telegraph and telephone. The AP's operation therefore "clearly constitutes interstate and foreign commerce." The Court had made it clear in prior decisions, the government argued, "that there is nothing special or peculiar in the standard communication businesses. Their inclusion in the concept of commerce is based on the broad principle laid down by Chief Justice Marshall, that commerce is 'intercourse' and that the 'transmission of intelligence' across the state lines, is, in its nature, a form of intercourse or commerce among the States."

The government attorneys next turned to John W. Davis' argument that the work of Morris Watson preceded interstate commerce and was therefore of a local nature just as production was generally local in nature affecting commerce only indirectly. The government argued in response that news flowed into the New York office of the AP in interstate and foreign commerce, was rewritten and edited by editorial employees such as Watson, and quickly distributed throughout the country. The rewriting and editing that was performed by editorial employees, the government contended, did not constitute a break or cessation of interstate commerce but was an activity that occurred in the flow of commerce and was an activity essential to the continuance of the flow of interstate communication of news by the AP. The government argued:

> The work done upon the news by the editorial employees is an important, and indeed an integral and indivisible part of the function of petitioner's world-wide enterprise for the collection and transmission of news. To say that "the analogy is exact between these employees and the employees of a manufacturing plant engaged in transforming the raw materials into a finished article" is to distort the long accepted sense of those words and invokes an analogy entirely unfitted to a business which describes itself as devoted to the accurate, impartial, and speedy gathering, exchange, and transmission of news.

Given the clearly interstate nature of the AP's operations, the question then became one of whether a congressional attempt to prevent labor disputes that would interrupt the AP's interstate communication of news was a valid exercise of the commerce power. And this question, the government contended, was settled beyond doubt by the *Texas & New Orleans Railroad* case (1930) in which the Court had sustained as valid under the Commerce Clause the Railway Labor Act of 1926 that was directed at the prevention of labor disputes interruptive of interstate rail transportation.

> That industrial disputes in an industry or business engaged in interstate commerce may and very frequently do burden and interrupt the flow of . . . commerce, is a fact of common knowledge. A strike or lockout ordinarily means a complete or partial suspension of business. That such an effect is so direct and substantial as to be within the scope of Congressional power has

been settled by *Texas & New Orleans R. Co.* v. *Brotherhood of Railway Clerks.* . . .

The fact that the *Texas & New Orleans Railroad* case dealt with interstate railroads did not mean that the principle it established was inapplicable to other forms of interstate commerce, the government contended, since "industrial strife threatening the operation of various other forms of commercial intercourse among the States, such as motor or water transportation, pipe lines, freight agency services, and communication by wireless, telephone, telegraph or radio, would directly affect interstate commerce and hence fall within Congressional power to mitigate or eliminate." Finally, although as recently as the *Carter* case (1936) the Court had held the employee-employer relationship to be "local" in nature, the government argued nonetheless that while "it be said that the right to join a labor organization is, standing alone, a local matter, that right may be protected by Congress where its protection will assist in maintaining the orderly conduct of interstate commerce, and in furthering the peaceful settlement of disputes which threaten it."

Charles Fahy thus summarized the government's position in the *Associated Press* case in the oral argument before the Court:

> With the power to regulate [interstate commerce] goes the responsibility of adopting reasonable means to protect it, and it has been found and it cannot be controverted, and it is not controverted, that the denial of [the right to organize and bargain collectively] leads to burdens and obstructions to interstate commerce.
>
> May those burdens and obstructions be prevented by the law, by the protection that this Court afforded under the railroad legislation, to these liberties of the employees, so that the controversy over them may cease to be the cause of these recurrent and ever-devastating obstructions to commerce? If that may not be done, are we faced with the situation that these rights must go on being fought for through industrial strife? That is the alternative, because, as this Court has said, the rights are essential. They

cannot be abandoned. They are necessary. They have long been recognized.

May they be protected by law, or must the employees be left to the protection of them only through industrial controversy leading to the burdens and obstructions to commerce which this statute seeks to avoid?

It is submitted that when the separate provisions of the statute itself are analyzed it will be found that they are reasonable, that they are not arbitrary or capricious, that they go no further than is reasonably necessary to accomplish the purpose of Congress, that they place no undue limitation upon the full freedom of the employer, and that the statute emerges as a reasonably well designed plan to afford the protection to interstate commerce which it was the object of Congress to achieve.

It is respectfully submitted that the circuit court, in the reasons that it gave for sustaining the order in this case, and in its decree sustaining the order, was correct, and its decree should be affirmed.

In the *Jones & Laughlin* case, the government counsel reiterated the contention that the act was intended to apply only to those businesses within the reach of Congress' commerce power, and therefore the act was clearly valid although its application to particular businesses by the NLRB might not be valid. Relying on the *Texas & New Orleans Railroad* case (1930), the government then argued that that case clearly established the validity and appropriateness of a statute guaranteeing the right to organize and bargain collectively as a congressional regulation of commerce. The *Texas & New Orleans Railroad* case, the government argued, could be distinguished from the *Jones & Laughlin* case "only upon a showing that industrial strife on the agencies of transportation can reasonably be expected to be more injurious to interstate commerce than industrial strife in an interstate enterprise." The government pointed out that a strike on the Pittsburgh & Lake Erie Railroad, 97 percent of whose shipments moved in or out of the Jones & Laughlin Aliquippa plant, could be regulated by the Congress because the railroad was clearly operating in interstate commerce. A strike at the Aliquippa plant, the government argued, would:

> . . . also obstruct the receipt and shipment of [Jones & Laughlin's] materials and products not only over the Pittsburgh & Lake Erie Railroad, but also over every other type of carrier which transports articles to and from [Jones & Laughlin's] plant. Indeed, it is true that a strike of the employees on the Pittsburgh & Lake Erie might result in only a very slight obstruction to interstate commerce if [Jones & Laughlin] could arrange to receive its materials and to ship its products by water, motor lines, or other carriers, while a strike among the employees of Jones & Laughlin at Aliquippa would completely stop all interstate commerce into and out of that plant.

A strike at the Aliquippa plant would thus be more disruptive of interstate commerce, the government argued, than a strike on an interstate carrier clearly subject to congressional regulation under the principle of the *Texas & New Orleans Railroad* case (1930); and therefore if the prevention of disruption of interstate rail traffic by congressional protection of the right to organize and bargain collectively was a valid regulation under the Commerce Clause, so too was such a regulation when extended to Jones & Laughlin's Aliquippa plant where a strike would be even more disruptive of interstate commerce.

The government attorneys next turned to the problem of demonstrating from essentially historical data that strikes in manufacturing or production industries, including the steel industry, had as devastating effects on interstate commerce as strikes in such clearly interstate industries as the railroads. From the steel industry's own publications, for example, the government demonstrated that the 1919 strike in steel had had a generally paralyzing effect upon the interstate steel market. Steel company representatives ceased to take orders for steel products and deliveries were delayed or prevented from being made altogether; the general business of interstate buying and selling steel products simply ceased while the strike remained effective.

A strike at the Jones & Laughlin Aliquippa plant, the government thus argued:

> . . . would mean the complete cessation of business, not merely the cessation of production. Materials in the amount of more than 200 freight cars per day would cease coming into the plant; the business of the Pittsburgh & Lake Erie Railroad at Aliquippa would be curtailed 97 percent; [Jones & Laughlin's] enormous lake and river traffic in ore, coal and steel products would come to a halt. The functional coherence of the entire enterprise would be destroyed. The dispute might involve a number of plants or even the whole industry. Employees not engaged in production would be apt to become active participants through sympathetic action. Markets would be disrupted. No business commitments could be made. Orders would be curtailed, and if given could not be filled. Movements and trading would stop. The effect upon commerce would be direct, immediate and substantial.

The NLRA could thus be validly applied to the labor relations of Jones & Laughlin's production employees at the Aliquippa plant because of the substantial effect upon commerce of a strike by such employees. In *United Mine Workers* v. *Coronado Coal Company* (1922), the Court had held that while mining was production and not commerce a strike by miners could still be reached by Congress under the Commerce Clause if "the obstruction to mining is intended to restrain commerce in it or had necessarily such a direct, material, and substantial effect to restrain it that the intent reasonably must be inferred." Citing the *Coronado Coal Company* case and similar cases in which the Court had sustained the application of the antitrust laws to strikes and boycotts by labor, the government argued that a strike at the Jones & Laughlin plant at Aliquippa would either involve an intent to obstruct interstate commerce in steel products or the effect upon commerce in such products would be so substantial that such intent could reasonably be inferred. Ironically, then, the cases in which organized labor had felt the courts had so unfairly applied the antitrust acts to it were utilized by the government in the *Jones & Laughlin* case as precedents supporting the power of Congress under the Commerce Clause to protect the right to organize and bargain collectively in production industries.

In addition to the antitrust cases involving labor, the government relied even more heavily in the *Jones & Laughlin* case upon the stream of commerce cases—*Swift* (1905), *Stafford* (1922), and *Olsen* (1923). Since the Court in those cases had upheld congressional power under the Commerce Clause to regulate activities admittedly local in nature that had the effect of obstructing or burdening a well defined flow or stream of interstate commerce, the government sought to designate labor disputes in production enterprises as local incidents in the stream of commerce which also had burdensome or obstructive effects on commerce. Jones & Laughlin, the government said, was:

> . . . engaged in a highly integrated interstate enterprise involving ownership of sources of supply, interstate transportation facilities, manufacturing plants, and outlets for distribution. This enterprise is dependent upon a great movement of iron ore, coal and limestone along well-defined paths to the steel mills, thence through them, and thence, in the form of steel products, into the consuming centers of the country—a "definite and well understood course of business." *Stafford* v. *Wallace*. . . . Industrial strife in the focal point of this stream—the Aliquippa plant— would cripple the entire movement of this great stream or flow of commerce.

Earl Reed had argued that the Court had held in the *Carter* (1936) and *Schechter* (1935) cases that the concept of the stream of commerce did not apply to activities which occurred after interstate movement had ceased entirely, never to resume, or when interstate commerce ceased for long periods of time, such as in manufacturing or conversion of raw materials into finished products that were then shipped in interstate commerce. Indeed, Justice Sutherland's statement on this point in the *Carter* case appeared to doom the NLRA as far as its application to production enterprises was concerned. It was nowhere suggested in the stream of commerce cases, Sutherland had said, "that the interstate commerce power extended to the growth or production of the things which, after production, entered the flow. If the court had held that the raising of cattle, which were involved in the Swift & Co. case, including the wages paid and working conditions of the herders and others employed in the business, could be regulated by Congress, that decision and decisions holding similarly would be in point. . . ."

In the *Jones & Laughlin* case the government argued that the Court had sanctioned congressional regulation of essentially manufacturing or production activities in upholding the Packers and Stockyards Act in *Stafford* v. *Wallace* (1922). The act had been upheld in the *Stafford* case as it applied to the purchase and sale of livestock for slaughter within a state, the processing of it into fresh meat, and its shipment in interstate commerce. "The Court thus recognized," the government argued, "that stoppage for purposes of processing in the packing plant, involving a definite interruption in the physical movement and a very distinct transformation in the nature of the commodity, did not cause a break in the 'stream' or 'current' of commerce in the constitutional sense." And if Congress could reach burdensome or obstructive activities or practices related to the processing of meat that affected commerce, Congress could similarly regulate labor disputes occurring in the Jones & Laughlin Aliquippa plant that would substantially affect the flow or stream of raw materials into the plant and the steel products out of the plant in interstate commerce.

Operations in meat packing plants, the government thus argued:

> . . . are as essentially manufacturing as are the operations at Aliquippa. It is common knowledge that meat packing involves a very extensive transformation in the nature of the commodity; this

is fully brought out in the authorities upon which the Court relied in the *Stafford* case. There, as here, the essential purpose of the processing operation is not merely to facilitate the flow of commerce, but also to halt it and to transform the commodities in question into things considerably different, by manufacturing or processing operations of varying degrees of complexity. Indeed, due to the seasonal character of the supply of raw materials and the stable demand for meat products, with a consequent necessity for much storage, and to the necessary slowness of many of the operations in the meat-packing industry, such as chilling, curing and smoking, the delays and stoppages of the flow of products in that industry are frequently much longer than those in the operations of [Jones & Laughlin]. . . . The relationship of industrial strife, at [Jones & Laughlin's] Aliquippa plant to [Jones & Laughlin's] entire interstate enterprise is no less direct than that of local practices in the livestock industry at the point where the commodities are halted . . . and go through extensive processing operations. Nor can it be said that the packers and stockyards illustration is peculiar because of the great public interest involved in the free and unburdened distribution of meat products in interstate commerce, for this alone does not create constitutional power where it does not otherwise exist. If such considerations were relevant, it could readily be demonstrated that uninterrupted commerce in the steel industry, of which [Jones & Laughlin's] enterprise forms one of the large units, is as important to our national commercial and economic life as is commerce in meat products.

This stream of commerce argument used by the government was the heart of its defense of the NLRA in the *Jones & Laughlin* case. If the Court was to be diverted from its rigid reliance upon the direct-indirect effects formula and the doctrine of dual federalism as evidenced in the *Schechter* (1935) and *Carter* (1936) cases, the stream of commerce cases furnished the strongest alternative conception of commerce available, and the government pushed this alternative to the fullest in the *Jones & Laughlin* case. Pressing their stream of commerce contentions before the Court orally, the government attorneys were subjected to the heaviest questioning they encountered from the bench. J. Warren Madden thus encountered close questioning from the Court conservatives on this point:

[MR. MADDEN]: I desire to return for the moment to a discussion of *Stafford* v. *Wallace* (258 U.S. 495), which is an analogy the Board has resorted to in the decision of its cases.

Can there be any doubt that industrial strife in a stockyard which would stop the stream of commerce through that stockyard would be a proper subject for the cognizance of the National Government?

JUSTICE VAN DEVANTER: Would you say that again, please?

MR. MADDEN: Can there be any doubt that labor trouble in a stockyard, which labor trouble stopped the flow of commerce through that stockyard, would constitutionally be a proper subject of control by the National Government?

JUSTICE MCREYNOLDS: If the men in that stockyard were employed at something which may not interfere with interstate commerce, how far would you go?

MR. MADDEN: There is always, of course, in considering these problems, just as there has been when this Court considered the labor cases under the Sherman Act, not merely the constitutional question of the limitation but the question of the wisdom and practicability of it.

JUSTICE MCREYNOLDS: I am asking you about the power. Does Congress have the power to say to these men—

MR. MADDEN: I should say that if they said to a man there, "You cannot quit your job," you would be in difficulties there with the thirteenth amendment to the Constitution. I should say that if you said to a group of men there, "You cannot enter into an agreement to quit your jobs, although individually you may quit them," there you would face no problem of constitutional power at all, but merely a problem of the wisdom of its exercise.

Now I should say that it would be unwise to so exercise the power unless you had first done all that you could by way of prevention of the difficulty.

JUSTICE MCREYNOLDS: We are not going to decide the wisdom of Congress. Did Congress in the *Stockyards case* interfere with the interstate commerce clause because they did not pay sufficient wages and say that they must pay each of them $10 a day?

MR. MADDEN: No; I should suppose not. I could imagine that there might be a sufficient connection between the wages and the labor troubles, thereby stopping the flow of commerce, but I see no such intimate connection whatever as there is between strikes and the flow of commerce.

The statistics which we rely upon here show that a very large number of strikes are not based at all upon problems of wages and hours and substantive conditions, but are based upon the desires of the men first to organize themselves into unions, so that they can speak to their employer with some authority with reference to their conditions. . . . It does seem to me that if the National Government really has the power to protect the flow of commerce through the stockyards, for example, by the meticulous regulation which it has imposed in the Packers and Stockyards Act, if the overcharge for the use of the stockyards of the amount of a few cents or a few dollars is really of interest to the National Government, then I cannot conceive of how some other activity which would stop the flow of commerce completely, instead of levying a little additional financial charge upon it, but which would stop it completely—I cannot conceive that would not be of equal interest to the National Government.

If you will indulge me, I want to read from Your Honor's own language in the—

JUSTICE SUTHERLAND: Is that the basis of your argument, that it completely stops the flow of commerce?

MR. MADDEN: That is the basis of my particular argument.

JUSTICE SUTHERLAND: In relation to this case?

MR. MADDEN: Yes. No; that is not all that there is to be said for this case. That is one of the arguments.

JUSTICE SUTHERLAND: In other words, that is the basis of the argument you are making now?

MR. MADDEN: Yes. . . . Now, if Your Honor please, it seems to me that the flow of commerce . . . in those stockyards cases was a flow of commerce not only through the stockyards but through the meat factories, through the packing plants. The consequence is that the analogy which we draw of the flow of raw materials into and through and the flow of finished products out of the steel mills seems to be a logical one.

JUSTICE SUTHERLAND: So far as the cattle are concerned, how far could you go? You say that that is an analogous situation?

MR. MADDEN: That is right.

JUSTICE SUTHERLAND: Taking it back, for instance, to the herder; suppose the herders raising cattle organized a union. Could Congress regulate that?

MR. MADDEN: I should say not, Your Honor. I should say that you have with reference to the commerce of the United States a problem somewhat similar—and certainly you have with reference to the extreme concept which this Court has used—you have a problem somewhat similar to that which you have with reference to physical streams of water. The water after it becomes a stream gets a wholly different sort of protection from what it gets when it is surface water or when it is percolating through the ground. At that time it is practically any man's property and it has very little protection from destruction. When it becomes a stream, however, it then comes under the scope of a different set of legal powers. . . .

Now it does seem to me that by your own authority the meat factory is in the stream of commerce. The stream of commerce flows through it. I can imagine no reason why the Government, which has not only the right but the duty to protect that great flow of commerce, cannot protect there as well as it can just before it reaches that point or just after it reaches that point. Indeed, it seems to me that the attempt of the National Government to protect its great streams of commerce is futile if there is somewhere along the stream a point where the hand of the Government is stayed and where stupid State regulation, or lack of regulation, may destroy the whole stream and which the Government has so carefully conserved up to that point, and which it is going to pick up and conserve so carefully beyond that point.

I just cannot see why the Government, which undertakes to protect this thing, should allow it to get out of control at some stage in the course of the stream and then perhaps permit it to be destroyed, which would be exactly what would happen, of course, to our enormous stream of raw materials coming into this steel mill and our finished products going out.

If labor trouble should stop this mill, there is no question but what transportation would stop, communication would stop, boats would be tied at their docks, interstate orders and shipments could not be made.

Now, why should the Government interest itself so meticulously in all of these things just before they enter the gates of this factory and then allow the whole work of conservation to be lost while they are inside it?

We no more assert that manufacturing is interstate commerce than did this Court in *Stafford* v. *Wallace* assert that meat packing or soap making or feeding hay to cows is interstate commerce. We merely assert that the Government, which has the responsibility, cannot have the factory gates slammed in its face and have it said to it, "Inside here you have lost your control, and whatever happens to your great stream of commerce is none of the National Government's business."

Solicitor General Stanley Reed also ran into difficulty in attempting to distinguish the *Carter* case (1936) from the *Jones & Laughlin* case on stream of commerce grounds:

[SOLICITOR GENERAL REED]: Here we have an act with a different purpose, aimed at a different evil. It is merely repetitious for me to say again that this act sought to control strikes which had the intent or the necessary effect of interfering with commerce, not the labor relations in and of themselves. The act is not, in other words, directed at a regulation of wages or hours, but at the elimination of the causes of those types of industrial disturbances which this Court has repeatedly said were within the power of Congress. Therefore, to us, the *Carter case* is not a bar to the consideration by this Court of the merits of this particular act. This act is aimed, within constitutional limits, at things that Congress has power to protect—the flow of interstate commerce and the carrying on of these great enterprises. So there is a distinction between the *Carter case,* which was directed at the control of wages and hours, and this case, which is directed at the removal of obstructions, or the removal of causes of obstructions, to the movement of interstate commerce.

It is not necessary that the *Carter case* should be overruled if this act is upheld. Nor is it necessary to think that if we can go this far in protecting commerce from obstructions because of the power to regulate strikes with intent or with the necessary effect of obstructing commerce, that we need open the door to go further into control of wages or hours or conditions of labor. It may well be that wages or hours or conditions of labor, as such, are beyond the power of Congress, because to interfere with them would be a violation of the due process clause; or we may say that wages and hours are so distinct and separate from interstate commerce that they do not have a direct effect upon it under any circumstances, while here the rights of labor which are protected fit directly into labor conditions which result directly in interferences and obstructions to interstate commerce.

I now pass from the problem of directly affecting commerce to that of the due process clause, insofar as this particular decree is concerned.

JUSTICE SUTHERLAND: Before you pass to that point, what is the primary effect of a strike in a steel mill? Is it not to simply curtail production?

MR. STANLEY REED: Certainly; that is one of the effects.

JUSTICE SUTHERLAND: Isn't that the primary effect, the immediate effect?

MR. STANLEY REED: Well, I should say it was the first effect. I do not mean to split hairs. Of course, that is one of the primary effects of it.

JUSTICE SUTHERLAND: That is the primary effect, to curtail production, and then the curtailment of production in its turn has an effect upon interstate commerce; isn't that true?

MR. STANLEY REED: As I understand it, no. The strike is not something that is a momentary change of, but instantaneously and at the same time that it stops production stops interstate commerce. It is a single thing that happens, and that stoppage of work stops interstate commerce right at that instant.

JUSTICE SUTHERLAND: It affects interstate commerce just as the cessation of work in a coal mine. The primary effect of that, as suggested in the *Carter case,* was to curtail the production, and then the secondary effect which came from the curtailment of production was the effect upon interstate commerce.

MR. STANLEY REED: Well, if we were undertaking to defend this act on the ground that Congress had the power to regulate labor conditions as such, I would fully agree with what Your Honor has said, but our contention is that Congress is not undertaking to regulate labor conditions as such; that it is undertaking to protect interstate commerce from situations that develop from those labor conditions, and that the causes which lead to these strikes with intent, and to strikes with the necessary effect, to interfere with interstate commerce are within the regulatory power of Congress.

JUSTICE SUTHERLAND: If by some means you curtail the production of wheat, the immediate effect, of course, is to curtail the production of wheat, and that in its turn has an effect upon interstate commerce. So would you say that Congress could step into that field and regulate the production of wheat under the commerce clause or under some other power?

MR. STANLEY REED: I am sure that what I would say would not bar Congress on it, but it seems to me that there is a great distinction between whether Congress can regulate production as such and whether Congress can regulate conditions which might interfere with the transportation of agricultural products after production.

I will say this: That although this act does not apply to agricultural production, probably, if Congress had undertaken to control situations that had for their purpose the stopping of such production, the same rule would apply. Fortunately, we do not have to reach that far in this case.

As the argument of Solicitor General Reed indicated, the government did not seek the reversal of the *Schechter* (1935) or *Carter* (1936) cases in the *Jones & Laughlin* case, but rather sought to distinguish them. Both the National Industrial Recovery Act and the Bituminous Coal Conservation Act which had been invalidated in the *Schechter* and *Carter* cases, the government contended, had been directed toward economic stabilization generally. The NLRA, on the other hand, was aimed at regulating only labor disputes within industry that would burden or obstruct interstate commerce. Also, the government said, the NLRA as applied to Jones & Laughlin "is concerned with activities which occur under circumstances closely related to a flow of commerce, and which directly affect that flow." In both the *Schechter* and *Carter* cases, the activities the government had sought to regulate had been entirely local activities. "In the Schechter case the flow of goods had ceased; in the Carter case the flow had not yet begun."

The Bituminous Coal Conservation Act had also contained provisions guaranteeing the right of labor to organize that had been invalidated by the Court in the *Carter* case (1936), a ruling that again appeared to doom the NLRA. Indeed, Justice Sutherland had said in the *Carter* case that:

> . . . the employment of men, the fixing of their wages, hours of labor and working conditions, the bargaining in respect of these things—whether carried on separately or collectively—each and all constitute intercourse for the purposes of production, not of trade. The latter is a thing apart from the relation of employer and employee, which in all producing occupations is purely local in character.

The government argued in the *Jones & Laughlin* case nonetheless that the collective bargaining provisions of the Bituminous Coal Act had been intimately tied to the overall provisions of the act that were directed at the stabilization of the mining industry, and they had not, therefore, been considered in isolation by the Court but rather as an inseparable part of a regulatory scheme which Congress lacked the power to enact. The government said:

> Thus the collective bargaining provisions, instead of being directly related to avoiding labor disputes interfering with interstate commerce, were subordinated to the main purpose of stabilization of the industry and were in fact the means through which one of the stabilizing factors—the establishment of uniform wages and hours —was to be effected.

The government's argument distinguishing the *Schechter* (1935) and *Carter* (1936) cases from the *Jones & Laughlin* case thus permitted room for maneuver and a line of retreat to the Justices that would allow them to avoid at least some of the embarrassment an outright reversal of those cases would have entailed. In view of the court-packing fight, an openly avowed reversal of the *Carter* and *Schechter* cases could hardly be expected, and the government's argument in the *Jones & Laughlin* case allowed room for a more oblique movement by the Court away from the principles in those cases. Indeed, this could be said of the entire argument of the government on the Commerce Clause in the *Jones & Laughlin* case; the government was not seeking a full retreat from the direct-indirect effects formula and the doctrine of dual federalism but rather a shifting of emphasis by the Court from those principles to the principles embodied in the stream of commerce cases.

LIBERTY OF CONTRACT ARGUMENTS

The government attorneys, however, also had to hurdle the doctrine of liberty of contract under the Due Process Clause of the Fifth Amendment—especially the principles enunciated by the Court in *Adair* v. *United States* (1908) and *Coppage* v. *Kansas* (1915). If the Court were to hold that the government was still barred under the doctrine of liberty of contract from interfering with the right of employers to hire and fire at will, then the NLRA was invalid on due process grounds no matter how persuasive the government's Commerce Clause arguments might be. The status of the *Adair* and *Coppage* cases had of course been murky since the *Texas & New Orleans Railroad* case (1930). In that case Chief Justice Hughes had held that the *Adair* and *Coppage* cases were "inapplicable" to the question of the validity of the Railway Labor Act of 1926. Both John W. Davis in the *Associated Press* case and Earl Reed in the *Jones & Laughlin* case argued that the NLRA was invalid on liberty of contract grounds. "The need (if need there be)," Davis thus argued, "for government protection of collective action on the part of employees is not in itself an exceptional circumstance which will justify an invasion of the normal right to property and liberty of contract. This was squarely decided in *Adair* v. *United States.* . . ." And Earl Reed arguing orally before the Court on behalf of Jones & Laughlin also asserted invasion of liberty of contract as a principal reason for the NLRA's invalidity under the Constitution:

> We raised also before the Board, and now, the question of the violation of the fifth amendment by this decision. The case of *Adair* v. *United States* (208 U.S. 161) decided flatly that a man had a right to hire whom he wished, and that a statute which forbade the discharge of an employee for union activities was unconstitutional.
>
> The same substantive decision was made in *Coppage* v. *Kansas.* . . .
>
> The posting of [a notice that Jones & Laughlin would not discriminate against union members] in the mill of Jones & Laughlin Steel Corporation would have meant that all discipline and control over the men in that organization was gone. The restoration of 10 men was a vastly more important thing than the wages involved. If it were announced, if it were known, as it would be, to 22,000 employees, that 10 men who had been discharged over a period of 6 months, who belonged to the union, had to be taken back and put back to work and had their positions, and could not be discharged except upon a hearing before the Labor Board, all freedom of contract, all right to manage your own business, is gone.
>
> Those men, if that be the law, if they can come back into this organization and go back to work for us, have a civil service status. They stand differently from any other employee in our employ, because they cannot be discharged without a hearing.
>
> Suppose their department shuts down. I suppose we have to go back to the Labor Board and ask to reopen this decree and show that they would not have had work if they had been working. Suppose they are tendered some other work that they do not want. In one of these discharge cases the man thought he was not equal to handling the machine that he had and he asked for something else, and in another a man had been absent a great many times.

Under this decree this money judgment goes into effect and we pay them these back wages indefinitely, apparently.

Suppose we want to transfer him to another department. Then I guess we have got to go to the Labor Board and show them that we have good ground for transferring that man and we want the thing modified so that we can put him in another department.

Suppose there is a question of promotion. There is no reason for not applying it to promotions. Daily they are making complaints that a man promoted is a nonunion man and therefore it was a discrimination. I suppose every time we wanted to promote a man we would have to go back to the Board and ask them to reopen this decree and let us promote the man.

Now, an employer has to have discretion. He cannot always give a reason for a discharge. There are times when sabotage occurs, times when there is a theft, and he cannot fasten the responsibility. There are men who are just a disorganizing influence and have to be transferred. There are men who have no promise of ability, who cannot either maintain or operate a machine, or who are a constant menace to their fellow employees. Is the discretion of the management to be reviewed every time the man discharged happens to be a union man? Here are 22,000 employees, and 10 of them over 6 months discharged that happen to be members of the union, and we are hauled into court and have to [try] to show why we discharged those 10 men. Is that an interference with the right of freedom of contract? Is that an interference with the right to run our business as we think best?

It seems to be that the Government's argument comes down to an economic argument. "It would be a good thing," says Mr. Madden, "if the Federal Government could control the labor relations of industry." But that is not the law, and never has been. He may think that the States are handling it "stupidly," as he says. He may think that a centralized government in which the Federal Government controls all of the labor relations of industry is desired. That is not the law and never has been.

Both Davis and Reed distinguished the *Texas & New Orleans Railroad* case (1930) on the grounds that the district court, whose order had been upheld by the Supreme Court in that case, was not enforcing the provisions of the Railway Labor Act that protected the right to organize but was rather enforcing those provisions of the act that provided for mediation of labor disputes. The court order involved in the case was thus not directed at the employer's right to hire and fire, but was directed at restoring the status quo so that the mediation machinery of the Railway Labor Act could be utilized to settle the dispute.

The government, on the other hand, argued that the *Adair* (1908) and *Coppage* (1915) cases were completely undermined by the *Texas & New Orleans Railroad* case (1930) and that they could not therefore be invoked as grounds for the invalidity of the NLRA under the Due Process Clause. "The *Adair* and *Coppage* cases need not be extensively analyzed here," the government argued in its *Associated Press* brief. "It is sufficient to say that both decisions were vigorously urged by the carrier in the *Texas & New Orleans* case. The facts of the latter case are so similar to those of the case at bar that the earlier cases, if inapplicable there, cannot be applicable here."

FREEDOM OF THE PRESS

John W. Davis also argued that the NLRA as applied to the Associated Press violated the freedom of the press guaranteed by the First Amendment. Freedom of the press, he asserted, was destroyed if the press employer was not completely free to determine who should work for him in the capacity of writing the news. Since the NLRA interfered with this right of the employer it invaded the First Amendment guarantee of freedom of the press. The government countered this argument by pointing out that the NLRA did not prevent the Associated Press from firing an editorial employee because he was biased or otherwise unqualified to write or report the news. The NLRA, the government said, "goes no further than the requirement that [the AP] refrain from interfering with its employees in their self-organization for collective bargaining, and consequently that [the AP] refrain from discharging an employee for the reason that he belongs to a labor organization."

A NATIONAL ECONOMY CONFRONTS THE OLD CONSTITUTION

The arguments in the *Jones & Laughlin, Associated Press, Fruehauf, Friedman-Harry Marks,* and *Washington, Virginia and Maryland Coach Company* cases testing the validity of the NLRA involved essentially the clash of constitutional theories fashioned in an earlier day and reflecting economic conditions of another century with theories that reflected the complexity and interdependence of the modern American economy. The ironic lack of realism in the direct-indirect effects formula and the doctrine of dual federalism is graphically illustrated by the fact that under the principles they embodied the validity of the NLRA seemed clearest in its application to the Associated Press and to the Washington, Virginia and Maryland Coach Company, a small and almost insignificant interstate business. And the validity of the NLRA was gravely in doubt under the prevailing principles of the Commerce Clause in its application to the Jones & Laughlin Steel Corporation, the fourth largest producer of steel in the nation. This was because Jones & Laughlin was engaged in "production" which had only "indirect" effects upon commerce, or which was reserved to the states for regulation under the Tenth Amendment, while the Washington, Virginia and Maryland Coach Company was clearly an "interstate" business.

The ironic effect of the prevailing principles of constitutional interpretation was further emphasized in the oral argument by the counsel for Fruehauf Trailer Company before the Court:

> This business began back in 1897. Mr. August Fruehauf had a little blacksmith shop and a wagon shop; they almost went together in those days. The picture of it is in the record as exhibit

2, which shows this little shop, just a typical blacksmith shop. He went along on the even tenor of his ways, and the automobile, the motorcar came along, and he conceived the idea that, along with the sort of business he was qualified to do, he could make a trailer to be put on behind the truck, with two wheels, or to be put on behind a tractor, with four wheels, and that he could increase the usefulness of the truck and the tractor a great deal, and thereby he could build up a business.

So he started in at that. He had a number of sons coming along and he could make opportunity for them. He could also take in his sons-in-law. So he got the business up to the point where this inquiry came along—700 men employed in production and about 200 others. They had never had any labor troubles, never in the world. . . .

Your Honors will observe that the question which we have here is really the old question of States' rights as against national power. And I want in that connection to call attention to the fact, and spend a few minutes on it, that we are here dealing with a part of the automotive industry, an industry which is peculiar to the State of Michigan. The plants of the State of Michigan could supply the world if there were none other. They have that capacity. It is all located there. It is essentially a local industry. . . .

The activity and growth of the Fruehauf Co., as I have outlined it here, are not peculiar to the Fruehauf Co. They are typical of the automotive industry, very typical. You could say the same thing of the Dodges, Fords, Olds, Chrysler, Nash, and so on. They all came up in the same way.

Now, I submit that it was for the State of Michigan to say whether the automobile industry would be developed in the State of Michigan under excessive restrictions or would be developed under freedom. The State of Michigan has permitted the automobile industry to develop and it has developed, to be one of the strongest industries in the country, proven by its recent comeback from the depression leading all other businesses, because it has been known that it has been free. It has been the outstanding example of good employer-employee relations, with wages the highest of any businesses, and there never has been any trouble. Counsel who just spoke called attention to all the statistics and the history of strikes, and so forth, which the Government has in its briefs. They go away back. I make another objection to their

statistics. Let them bring in statistics as to the automobile industry and let us see whether they will show about interruptions and
disturbances, whether it is local or whether it is interstate.

It thus seemed from this argument that under the Commerce Clause the Fruehauf Trailer Company was to be considered as if it were still a small blacksmith shop having only
state or local importance, rather than a company employing
over seven hundred men and utilizing raw materials drawn
from numerous other states in interstate commerce. And the
Court was also being asked to ignore the fact that at the time
such an argument was being made to it sit-down strikes by
members of the United Automobile Workers were paralyzing
a major segment of the automobile industry, creating a crisis
not of local or state but of national dimensions.

Charles Wyzanski, summing up for the government at the
close of the oral arguments, also caught the irony of the Fruehauf counsel's remarks:

> Before I conclude I want to say one very general word. I
> thought the argument of the respondent in the *Fruehauf case* was
> a rather interesting one, in which he pointed out that in the State
> of Michigan were almost all the automobile factories, and it was
> only necessary for the State of Michigan to determine the policy in
> order to have the commerce of the country protected. I am not
> going to refer in detail to facts which all of us know at the present
> day. I merely point out that it is well recognized that there is a
> national public interest in this subject, so great that no dispute of
> the character which he envisages could possibly be adjusted with-
> out the cooperation both of the parties themselves and of public
> authorities, and that in the past on many occasions the Federal
> authorities have found it necessary to intervene. I do not suggest
> that the Federal Government can build up its *de jure* power
> merely by a series of particular *de facto* interventions in disputes,
> but I do say that the problem itself is obviously of such national
> character, at least in some of its instances, as to justify the
> intervention of Congress, and I contend that where two colossal
> forces are standing astride the stream of commerce threatening to

disrupt it, it cannot be that this Government is without power to provide for the orderly procedure by which the dispute may be adjusted without interruption to the stream of commerce.

It was 4:08 p.m., February 11, 1937. The fate of the NLRA, and with it the future course of American constitutional development, was in the hands of the Court.

THE COURT RETREATS

Following the oral arguments in the cases testing the constitutionality of the NLRA, there was a delay of two months while the Court digested the briefs and arguments in the cases. On March 29 reporters and spectators packed the courtroom hoping to hear the opinions in the NLRA cases, but instead they heard the Court's opinions in West Coast Hotel v. Parrish, 300 U.S. 379 (1937).

THE *PARRISH* CASE

The *Parrish* case involved the constitutionality of a Washington minimum wage statute almost identical with the New York statute held invalid by the Court in the *Morehead* case (1936). The appeal in the case had been filed in August 1936, and the Court had considered the question of whether to grant a hearing in the *Parrish* case during early October. In conference, Justices Van Devanter, Sutherland, Butler, and McReynolds voted to invalidate the statute summarily on the basis of the *Adkins* (1923) and *Morehead* cases, but since the Court was being asked in the *Parrish* case to reverse the *Adkins* case, Justice Roberts voted in favor of giving the *Parrish* case a hearing. "I am not sure I gave my reason," Roberts later explained, "but it was that in the appeal in the *Parrish* case the authority of *Adkins* was definitely assailed and the Court was asked to reconsider and overrule it. Thus, for the first time, I was confronted with the necessity of facing the soundness of the *Adkins* case." The conservatives expressed their surprise at Roberts' action and someone asked, "What is the matter with Roberts?" The case was argued orally before the Court on December 16 and 17, and when it was taken up in conference on December 19, Roberts voted to uphold the minimum wage statute. Because of the illness of Justice Stone, the vote was four to four, but Stone returned to the Court and voted to uphold the statute on February 6, the day following Roosevelt's attack on the Court.

The Court thus announced its five to four decision in the *Parrish* case on March 29. Abandoning the narrow ground upon which he had dissented in the *Morehead* case (1936), Chief Justice Hughes in the majority opinion overruled the *Adkins* case (1923). He said:

> In each case, the violation alleged by those attacking minimum wage regulation for women is deprivation of freedom of contract. What is this freedom? The Constitution does not speak of freedom of contract. It speaks of liberty and prohibits deprivation of liberty without due process of law. In prohibiting that deprivation, the Constitution does not recognize an absolute and uncontrollable liberty. . . . The exploitation of a class of workers who are in an unequal position with respect to bargaining and thus are relatively defenseless against the denial of a living wage is not only detrimental to their health and well-being, but casts a direct burden for their support on the community. . . . The community is not bound to provide what is in effect a subsidy for unconscionable employers. The community may direct its law-making power to correct the abuse which springs from the selfish disregard of the public interest.

The conservative bloc, however, charged in its dissent that the majority had amended the Constitution by judicial decree. To say, Sutherland wrote, "that the words of the Constitution mean today what they did not mean when written—that is, that they do not apply to a situation now to which they would have applied then—is to rob that instrument of the essential element which continues it in force as the people have made it until they, and not their official agents, have made it otherwise."

The Court's decision in the *Parrish* case (1937) of course created a great public furor since it appeared that Roberts had switched his position since the decision in the *Morehead* case (1936). Roberts' behavior was attributed to the court-packing fight, and New Dealers were soon calling Roberts' vote in the *Parrish* case "the switch in time that saved nine." As we have seen, however, Roberts' vote to sustain the minimum wage statute in the *Parrish* case had been cast on December 19, 1936, before Roosevelt introduced the court-packing plan. Roberts' behavior may be attributed to the overwhelming re-election of Roosevelt in 1936 or the popular revulsion to the *Morehead* decision, but not to the court-packing plan. The crucial turning point in constitutional development and switches in positions by both Justice Roberts and Chief Justice Hughes came not in the *Parrish* case but in the *Jones & Laughlin* case.

On April 10, 1937, the annual Gridiron dinner was held in Washington, a traditional affair at which the press pokes fun at prominent national figures and satirizes national issues. The featured skit at the dinner centered on the Supreme Court and the court-packing fight. In part of the skit a messenger from the "President" arrived at a packed, fifteen member "Supreme Court" bearing newly passed legislation. "Get a move on and hold these laws constitutional," the messenger ordered the "Chief Justice." "The President wants them. It took him almost two hours this morning to get them through

Congress. There's a crisis." "But how do I know what's in 'em?" the "Chief Justice" asked. "You don't have to know what's in 'em," the messenger replied. "Even Congress doesn't know that. You don't think you're better than Congress, do you?" The "Chief Justice" then addressed his fellow "Justices," "Gentlemen of the court, get out your rubber stamps! And, above all, keep your minds off John Marshall!"

THE NLRA DECISIONS

In the audience at the Gridiron dinner were Chief Justice Hughes and Justices Stone and McReynolds. On the following day Hughes celebrated his seventy-fifth birthday, and at noon on April 12 he parted the curtains behind the bench and led the Justices into the courtroom. After the Justices were seated, the Chief Justice gave a slight nod to Justice Roberts who began reading the opinion of the Court in the *Associated Press* case. "The silent intake of spectators' breaths," it was reported, "all but caused a vacuum in the courtroom."

The *AP* Case

After reciting the facts in Associated Press v. NLRB, 301 U.S. 103 (1937), and describing the nature of the AP's operations, Roberts declared that these "operations involve the constant use of channels of interstate and foreign communication. . . . They amount to commercial intercourse, and such intercourse is commerce within the meaning of the Constitution. Interstate communication of a business nature, whatever the means of such communication, is interstate commerce regulable by Congress under the Constitution." To the AP's contention that its editorial employees were not engaged in commerce, Roberts, citing such cases as the *Texas & New Orleans Railroad* case (1930), replied that "it is obvious that strikes or labor disturbances amongst this class of employees would have as direct an effect upon the activities of petitioner as similar disturbances amongst those who operate the teletype machines or as a strike amongst the employees of telegraph lines over which petitioner's messages travel."

Having completely sustained the government's position on the commerce question in the *Associated Press* case, Roberts then proceeded to deny the claim that the NLRA as applied to the AP violated freedom of the press. He said:

> We think the contention not only has no relevance to the circumstances of the instant case but is an unsound generalization. The ostensible reason for Watson's discharge, as embodied in the records of the petitioner, is "solely on the grounds of his work not being on a basis for which he has shown capability." The petitioner did not assert and does not claim that he had shown bias in the past. It does not claim that by reason of his connection with the union he will be likely, as the petitioner honestly believes, to show bias in the future. The actual reason for his discharge, as shown by the unattacked finding of the Board, was his Guild activity and his agitation for collective bargaining. The statute does not preclude a discharge on the ostensible grounds for the petitioner's action; it forbids discharge for what has been found to be the real motive of petitioner. . . . The restoration of Watson to his former position in no sense guarantees his continuance in petitioner's employ. The petitioner is at liberty, whenever occasion may arise, to exercise its undoubted right to sever his relationship for any cause that seems to it proper save only as a punishment for, or discouragement of, such activities as the act declares permissible.

Following the reading of his opinion in the *Associated Press* case, Roberts read the Court's brief, unanimous opinion upholding the NLRA as applied in Washington, Virginia and Maryland Coach Company v. NLRB, 301 U.S. 142 (1937). Justice Sutherland, joined by Van Devanter, McReynolds, and Butler, dissented from the majority opinion in the *Associated Press* case on the grounds that the act's application to news services violated the freedom of the press guaranteed by the First Amendment. "If the freedom of the press does not include the right to adopt and pursue a policy without government restriction," Sutherland said, "it is a misnomer to call it freedom." The majority's decision, he contended, if pushed to its logical extreme, would give the American Newspaper Guild opportunity "to exercise a high degree of control over the character of the news service. Due regard for the constitutional guaranty requires that the publisher or agency of the publisher of news shall be free from restraint in respect to employment in the editorial force." In conclusion, Sutherland asked:

> Do the people of this land—in the providence of God, favored, as they sometimes boast, above all others in the plenitude of their liberties—desire to preserve those so carefully protected by the First Amendment . . . ? If so, let them withstand all *beginnings* of encroachment. For the saddest epitaph which can be carved in memory of a vanished liberty is that it was lost because its possessors failed to stretch forth a saving hand while yet there was time.

The *Jones & Laughlin* Decision

Having sustained the application of the NLRA to clearly interstate businesses the Court now faced the crucial question of whether the application of the act to manufacturing enterprises was constitutionally valid. Chief Justice Hughes now took the lead from Roberts and read the opinion of the majority in NLRB v. Jones & Laughlin Steel Corp., 301 U.S. 1 (1937), fully affirming the NLRB's approach to its manufacturing cases. The NLRA's grant of authority to the Board, Hughes said:

> . . . purports to reach only what may be deemed to burden or obstruct . . . commerce and, thus qualified, it must be construed as contemplating the exercise of control within constitutional bounds. It is a familiar principle that acts which directly burden or obstruct interstate or foreign commerce, or its free flow, are within the reach of the congressional power. Acts having that effect are not rendered immune because they grow out of labor disputes.

The right of employees to organize, the Chief Justice continued, was a "fundamental right" equal to that of employers to organize their businesses.

> Long ago, we stated the reason for labor organizations. We said they were organized out of the necessities of the situation; that a single employee was helpless in dealing with an employer; that he was dependent ordinarily on his daily wage for the maintenance of himself and family; that if the employer refused to pay him the wages that he thought fair, he was nevertheless unable to leave the employ and resist arbitrary and unfair treatment; that union was essential to give laborers opportunity to deal on an equality with their employer.

Hughes then reviewed the argument of Jones & Laughlin that its Aliquippa plant was engaged in manufacturing and was therefore beyond the reach of Congress under the Commerce Clause, and the government's argument in which it attempted to demonstrate that the stream of commerce cases were applicable to Jones & Laughlin's activities. "We do not find it necessary to determine whether these features of defendant's business," Hughes said, "dispose of the asserted analogy to the 'stream of commerce' cases."

> The instances in which that metaphor has been used are but particular, and not exclusive, illustrations of the protective power which the Government invokes in support of the present Act. The congressional authority to protect interstate commerce from burdens and obstructions is not limited to transactions which can be deemed to be an essential part of a "flow" of interstate or foreign commerce. Burdens and obstructions may be due to injurious action springing from other sources. The fundamental principle is that the power to regulate commerce is the power to enact "all appropriate legislation" for "its protection and advancement" . . . to adopt measures "to promote its growth and insure its safety" . . . "to foster, protect, control and restrain. . . ." That power is plenary and may be exerted to protect interstate commerce "no matter what the source of the dangers which threaten it. . . ." Although activities may be intrastate in character when separately considered, if they have such a close and

substantial relation to interstate commerce that their control is essential or appropriate to protect that commerce from burdens and obstructions, Congress cannot be denied the power to exercise that control. . . .

The question, then, was whether labor disputes in a manufacturing plant such as Jones & Laughlin's Aliquippa plant would threaten or obstruct interstate commerce sufficiently to justify congressional legislation that attempted to eliminate the causes of such disputes. The answer, Hughes said, was affirmative.

> Giving full weight to respondent's contention with respect to a break in the complete continuity of the "stream of commerce" by reason of respondent's manufacturing operations, the fact remains that the stoppage of those operations by industrial strife would have a most serious effect upon interstate commerce. In view of respondent's far-flung activities, it is idle to say that the effect would be indirect or remote. It is obvious that it would be immediate and might be catastrophic. We are asked to shut our eyes to the plainest facts of our national life and to deal with the question of direct and indirect effects in an intellectual vacuum. Because there may be but indirect and remote effects upon interstate commerce in connection with a host of local enterprises throughout the country, it does not follow that other industrial activities do not have such a close and intimate relation to interstate commerce as to make the presence of industrial strife a matter of the most urgent national concern. When industries organize themselves on a national scale, making their relation to interstate commerce the dominant factor in their activities, how can it be maintained that their industrial labor relations constitute a forbidden field into which Congress may not enter when it is necessary to protect interstate commerce from the paralyzing consequences of industrial war? We have often said that interstate commerce itself is a practical conception. It is equally true that interferences with that commerce must be appraised by a judgment that does not ignore actual experience.

The final hurdle for the NLRA, the Fifth Amendment liberty of contract issue, was scaled on the basis of the *Texas & New Orleans Railroad* case (1930). The Chief Justice again simply pointed out that the *Adair* (1908) and *Coppage* (1915) cases were not controlling. Hughes said:

> The Act does not interfere with the normal exercise of the right of the employer to select its employees or to discharge them. The employer may not, under cover of that right, intimidate or coerce its employees with respect to their self-organization and representation, and, on the other hand, the Board is not entitled to make its authority a pretext for interference with the right of discharge when that right is exercised for other reasons than such intimidation and coercion.

In brief opinions, the Chief Justice also sustained the Board's application of the NLRA in NLRB v. Fruehauf Trailer Co., 301 U.S. 49 (1937) and NLRB v. Friedman-Harry Marks Clothing Co., 301 U.S. 58 (1937). The Chief Justice, *The New York Times* reported, "appeared in splendid physical form, reading opinions for more than an hour in a strong, resonant voice and accentuating his words with many gestures." As in the *Associated Press* case, Justices Sutherland, Butler, Van Devanter, and McReynolds dissented, this time on both commerce and due process grounds. McReynolds delivered his dissent extemporaneously in the courtroom, heaping scorn on the majority's position in the manufacturing cases. "The field opened here [under the Commerce Clause]," McReynolds declared, "is wider than most of the citizens of the country can dream. The cause is so momentous, the possibilities for harm so great that we felt it our duty to expose the situation as we see it." The *Jones & Laughlin, Friedman-Harry Marks,* and *Fruehauf* cases all involved manufacturing establishments, McReynolds continued, and the "court has decided again and again within the last fifty years, and particularly in the last two years, that manufacturing is only incidentally related to interstate commerce and that Congress has no authority to interfere with manufacturing, operating as such. We supposed that was settled as much as anything can be settled." Citing the Friedman-Harry Marks Clothing Company as an example of the majority's exaggeration of the stream of commerce concept, McReynolds declared with a sarcastic drawl that the majority had sustained the argument that "this concern is in the stream-m-m-m-m of interstate commerce and that when this concern is shut up, the stream-m-m-m-m is blocked." Under this doctrine, he said, the marriage of "Mary Jones and John Smith" might be considered in the stream of commerce.

In his written dissent Justice McReynolds attacked the reasoning by which unfair labor practices in manufacturing enterprises were held by the majority to affect commerce, and declared that by this "chain of indirect and progressively remote events we finally reach the evil with which it is said the legislation under consideration undertakes to deal. . . . A more remote and indirect interference with interstate commerce," he said, "or a more definite invasion of the powers reserved to the states is difficult, if not impossible, to imagine." Relying on the *Adair* (1908) and *Coppage* (1915) cases, McReynolds described the right to contract as one which is:

> . . . fundamental and includes the privilege of selecting those with whom one is willing to assume contractual relations. This right is unduly abridged by the Act now upheld. A private owner is deprived of power to manage his own property by freely selecting those to whom his manufacturing operations are to be entrusted. We think this cannot lawfully be done in circumstances like those here disclosed.

THE UNIONIZATION OF THE STEEL INDUSTRY

While the *Jones & Laughlin* case was being litigated, momentous events had been occurring in the steel industry. After the CIO broke with the AFL one of its first concerns was the organization of the steel industry. Through a protracted series of negotiations, the CIO persuaded President Tighe of the Amalgamated Association of Iron, Steel and Tin Workers to confer his union's jurisdiction over the steel industry upon the CIO-sponsored Steel Workers Organizing Committee. Supported by a loan of $500,000 from the United Mine Workers, the SWOC was soon spending $45,000 per week and utilizing over a hundred full-time organizers in a drive to organize steel.

On June 19, 1936, the SWOC sent an organizer into Aliquippa, just after the loss of the *Jones & Laughlin* case by the NLRB in the court of appeals. The first SWOC organization meeting in Aliquippa was attended by only eighteen men, but throughout the summer of 1936 SWOC membership climbed steadily, as it was doing in the rest of the steel industry. The news of the Court's decision in the *Jones & Laughlin* case was received uproariously in Aliquippa. Asked what he thought of the decision, a Jones & Laughlin steel worker said, "When I hear Wagner Act went constitutional I happy like anything. I say, good, now Aliquippa become part of the United States." A parade of steel workers celebrating the decision proceeded up the main street of the city, with the discharged employees in the first two cars bearing signs reading, "We Are the Ten Men Fired for Union Activity by J & L, We Are Ordered Back to Work by the Supreme Court" and "The Workers of Aliquippa Are Now Free Men." The Court's decision came as the steel industry was staggering under the drive of the SWOC. Faced with the defection of the leaders of its company unions to the SWOC, U.S. Steel had begun negotiations with John L. Lewis in January 1937, and an agreement had been signed on March 3 which established the eight-hour day and forty-hour week and granted recognition to the SWOC.

This action of U.S. Steel was regarded as a sell-out by the heads of many steel corporations. Myron R. Taylor, the chairman of the board of U.S. Steel who had negotiated with Lewis, was ousted as chairman of the Iron and Steel Institute and replaced by Tom Girdler, head of Republic Steel. Thus "Little Steel," composed of Republic and other moderate-sized corporations, decided on a continued resistance to the SWOC, while Jones & Laughlin became a key target of the SWOC's organizational efforts. By May Jones & Laughlin began negotiations with Phillip Murray of the SWOC, but these broke down and on May 12 a strike was called by the SWOC against Jones & Laughlin. This strike in Aliquippa was described as being "virtually a civil upheaval" and more "a demonstration of political and economic independence on the part of the workers than a labor dispute."

On May 13 a leader of the Aliquippa strikers telegraphed President Roosevelt that unless an NLRB election was held, "we will take the law into our own hands at ten a.m., Saturday, May 15, 1937. You as President of these United States may be responsible for loss of life and property if you do not do your duty." The tense situation in Aliquippa was not helped by reports that Tom Girdler's Republic Steel had sent its gas pipe gang and almost all of its company police into Aliquippa during the crisis. The strike at Aliquippa had lasted only thirty-six hours when Jones & Laughlin signed a contract with the SWOC, and on May 20, in an NLRB election, the SWOC received 17,028 votes out of a total of 24,412 votes cast and became the exclusive bargaining agent of Jones & Laughlin's employees. Asked what he thought of the SWOC's organization of Jones & Laughlin, a steel worker replied that it was "worth twelve dollars a year [in union dues] to be able to walk down the main street of Aliquippa, talk to anyone you want about anything you like, and feel that you are a citizen."

THE REACTIONS TO THE COURT'S RETREAT

The liberals on the Supreme Court were as delighted with the *Jones & Laughlin* decision as the workers in Aliquippa. "Of course," Justice Stone wrote privately, "in order to reach the result which was reached in these cases last Monday, it was necessary for six members of the Court either to be overruled or to take back some things they subscribed to in the [*Carter Coal Company*] case. But as I did not join in those statements, I had nothing to take back." Chief Justice Hughes and Justice Roberts had indeed "taken back" some of their earlier views. In the previous year Roberts had joined the majority in the *Carter Coal Company* case which held that labor relations in production enterprises had only indirect effects on interstate commerce and were thus beyond the reach of the commerce power. And Chief Justice Hughes had declared in his partial dissent in that case that "if the people desire to give Congress the power to regulate industries within the States, and the relations of employers and employees in those industries, they are at liberty to declare their will in the appropriate manner, but it is not for the Court to amend the Constitution by judicial decree." The Constitution remained unamended in April 1937, but the Court in the *Jones & Laughlin* case had sustained the power of Congress "to regulate industries within the States and the relations of employers and employees in those industries. . . ." It is to both Hughes' and Roberts' credit, however, that when the forces of political and social unrest beat upon the Court in the spring of 1937, they did not feel bound to a rigid adherence to previous utterances in the hope of maintaining reputations for constitutional consistency. Despite his questionable wavering on some basic issues, it is to the credit of Hughes especially that when the Court met its most serious modern challenge he possessed the ability, both political and legal, to guide through the storm the institution which he headed.

Upon learning of the Court's decisions upholding the NLRA, however, Felix Frankfurter wired the President that after "today I feel like finding some honest profession to enter." The President nevertheless greeted the decisions enthusiastically. "We did it," he exclaimed. "I am very, very pleased. You ought to see [Attorney General] Homer Cummings, who's sitting with me now. He looks like the Cheshire cat that swallowed the canary. It's wonderful. I am convinced more than ever that the proposals for reform of the Court are warranted. It's the same four justices who have dissented all along that are against me this time—McReynolds, Butler, Sutherland and Van Devanter." And in a phone call to Speaker of the House Bankhead, congratulating the Speaker on his birthday, Roosevelt said, "It's been a pretty good day for all of us."

The Court's decisions sustaining the NLRA constituted a great personal victory for Senator Robert Wagner. Addressing a radio audience on the significance of the Court's decisions, Wagner stated that the Court had accepted the view that "our nation-wide social and economic system makes it imperative to treat that system on a national scale if the system is to be preserved at all. . . . In holding that what happens in our great manufacturing industries is of national import, the court has performed an act of industrial statesmanship ranking alongside the work done in the days of John Marshall."

During the reading of the Court's opinions sustaining the NLRA the government attorneys involved could hardly conceal their pleasure, and after the Court's adjournment, *The New York Times* reported that many declared that "the court had put a twentieth century dress on Marshall's dictum in the famous case of Gibbons v. Ogden, reversing the line it has taken in recent years." Chairman Warren Madden of the NLRB added that the Court's action meant "industrial peace."

Secretary of Labor Frances Perkins echoed the enthusiasm of the government attorneys in her appraisal of the NLRA decisions. The decisions in "the manufacturing cases," she said, "are of great significance. They illustrate conclusively that the Constitution is indeed broad enough to give Congress power to deal with our most pressing social and industrial problems. . . . [The Court] has done away with the principal cause of industrial unrest in America." Speaking for the AFL,

William Green agreed with Secretary Perkins. The Court's decisions had "deep significance," Green said, and would allow "labor to organize without fear of discrimination and persecution. A new impetus will be given to the organized labor movement."

THE DEFEAT OF THE COURT-PACKING PLAN

A substantial number of newspaper editorials pointed to the Supreme Court's decisions in the *Jones & Laughlin* and its companion cases as conclusive proof that the adoption of the court-packing plan was no longer necessary. This view was seconded by Senator Burton Wheeler, the leader of the opposition to Roosevelt's court plan. "The decisions," Wheeler declared, "were great. I feel now that there cannot be any excuse left for wanting to add six new members to the Supreme Court. The court enlargement proposal will certainly be defeated. A number of Senators have told me privately that if the court upheld the Labor Act, they did not see how they could vote for the court enlargement measure." Another Senator humorously suggested that the court-packing plan be shelved and the Congress instead direct its efforts at proposing a constitutional amendment "directing the President of the United States, whenever he finds it valuable to the public interest, to scare the Supreme Court of the United States."

John L. Lewis of the CIO, however, argued that the Court's "astonishing" decisions added justification for the passage of the court-packing plan. Lewis said:

> The quibblers of ancient Greece were intellectual sluggards as compared with our Supreme Court. Apparently the destiny of our Republic and the well-being of its population depend upon the legalistic whims and caprices of one man. . . . Yesterday the Guffey [Bituminous Coal Conservation] Act was struck down. today the Wagner Labor Relations Act is sustained. If today the Court is right, then yesterday, forsooth, the Court was wrong. The Court is as variable as the winds, and the people wonder how

long they are to be the victims of its instability. Obviously the situation needs change. The President's court plan is the immediate answer.

Although the Gallup Poll indicated a slight rise in the percentage of the public favorable to the President's court-packing plan following the decisions upholding the NLRA, by May 12 the Poll indicated that only thirty-one percent of the public then favored the plan. The President was determined to push the bill through the Congress, however, and refused to compromise. The congressional opposition to his plan, he said, was due to his telling Congress "I would not be a candidate again." The Court meanwhile sustained the Social Security Act on May 24,* confirming the power of Congress to tax and spend to promote the general welfare. And Congress had by this time passed a new retirement plan for the Justices that would allow them to retire from the Court rather than resign, with the result that the pensions of the Justices were protected by the constitutional provision prohibiting the reduction of their salaries while in office. Justice Van Devanter took advantage of this new retirement system and announced his retirement on May 18 effective at the end of the Court's term. Roosevelt had promised the first appointment to the Court to the Senate majority leader, Joseph Robinson of Arkansas, as a reward for pushing the court-packing bill through the Senate. Now Roosevelt sought a compromise that would allow him to appoint only one Justice per year for each one who had reached the retirement age but failed to retire, and he relied on the Senate's loyalty to Robinson for passage of this compromise.

On July 14, however, this hope also vanished when Robinson was found dead of a heart attack in his hotel room. It was then obvious that the court-packing proposal could not pass. Thus the court-packing fight ended, and with its termination,

* Steward Machine Co. v. Davis, 301 U.S. 548 (1937); Helvering v. Davis, 301 U.S. 619 (1937).

the coalition which had pushed through the domestic New Deal began to crack. Only one further major piece of New Deal domestic legislation, the Fair Labor Standards Act, would be passed, and it would have to be forced out of committee in the House by discharge petition. The court-packing fight had seen the beginning of the reestablishment of a conservative coalition in Congress which would mean the end of domestic reform.

THE COURT AND THE CONSTITUTION AFTER 1937

Roosevelt had continued to press for the court-packing plan because he undoubtedly felt that the narrow five to four margins by which the Court had reversed its position on many issues in 1937 might constitute only a temporary change in the Court's attitude. Soon after 1937, however, Roosevelt was able to appoint several new Justices, and by 1940 a majority of the Court was composed of Roosevelt appointees. (See Table 3.) The reversals of 1937 were therefore not temporary, but became a part of a permanent shift in the Court's interpreta-

TABLE 3
Changes in Membership of the Supreme Court
between 1937 and 1941

Membership of the Court in 1937	Left the Court in:	Replaced by:
Hughes	June 1941	Stone
Van Devanter	June 1937	Black
Sutherland	January 1938	Reed
Butler	November 1939	Murphy
McReynolds	February 1941	Byrnes
Brandeis	February 1939	Douglas
Stone	(Appointed Chief Justice, October 1941)	Jackson
Cardozo	July 1938	Frankfurter
Roberts		

tion of the Constitution in relation to governmental power to regulate the economy.

The use of the Due Process Clauses of the Constitution by the Court to invalidate legislation regulating the economic life of the nation was permanently abandoned after 1937, and doctrines such as liberty of contract ceased to be viable constitutional principles. Speaking in 1963, the Court thus acknowledged that there:

> . . . was a time when the Due Process Clause was used by this Court to strike down laws which were thought unreasonable, that is, unwise or incompatible with some particular economic or social philosophy. In this manner the Due Process Clause was used, for example, to nullify laws prescribing maximum hours for work in bakeries, Lochner v. New York . . . outlawing "yellow dog" contracts, Coppage v. Kansas . . . setting minimum wages for women, Adkins v. Children's Hospital. . . . This intrusion by the judiciary into the realm of legislative value judgments was strongly objected to at the time, particularly by Mr. Justice Holmes and Mr. Justice Brandeis. . . . The doctrine that prevailed in Lochner, Coppage, Adkins . . . and like cases—that due process authorizes courts to hold laws unconstitutional when they believe the legislature has acted unwisely—has long since been discarded. We have returned to the original constitutional proposition that courts do not substitute their social and economic beliefs for the judgment of legislative bodies, who are elected to pass laws.

Although in the *Jones & Laughlin* case the Court continued to utilize the terms "direct" and "indirect" in relation to the scope of congressional power under the Commerce Clause, the *Jones & Laughlin* case also signalled the abandonment of the direct-indirect effects formula and the doctrine of dual federalism as limitations upon the powers of Congress. Thus, in United States v. Darby Lumber Company, 312 U.S. 100 (1941), Justice Stone writing for a unanimous Court upheld the validity of the Fair Labor Standards Act, which regulated wages, hours, and child labor under the Commerce Clause. Stone specifically overruled *Hammer* v. *Dagenhart* (1918), the classic dual federalism case, holding that:

. . . the power of Congress over interstate commerce is not confined to the regulation of commerce among the states. It extends to those activities intrastate which so affect interstate commerce or the exercise of the power of Congress over it as to make regulation of them appropriate means to the attainment of a legitimate end, the exercise of the granted power of Congress to regulate interstate commerce.

Nor was the Tenth Amendment, the Court held, to be any longer considered as an independent limitation upon congressional power. The Court said:

There is nothing in the history of its adoption to suggest that it was more than declaratory of the relationship between the national and state governments as it had been established by the Constitution before the amendment or that its purpose was other than to allay fears that the new national government might seek to exercise powers not granted, and that the states might not be able to exercise fully their reserved powers. . . . From the beginning and for many years, the amendment has been construed as not depriving the national government of authority to resort to all means for the exercise of a granted power which are appropriate and plainly adapted to the permitted end.

Following the trend set in the *Jones & Laughlin* (1937) and *Darby* (1941) cases, the reconstituted "Roosevelt Court" in 1942 sustained the second Agricultural Adjustment Act's regulation of agricultural production in Wickard v. Filburn, 317 U.S. 111 (1942), taking the opportunity to repudiate past commerce principles and to enunciate the principles governing the modern scope of congressional power under the Commerce Clause. Justice Robert Jackson stated the Court's belief that "a review of the course of decision under the Commerce Clause will make plain . . . that questions of the power of Congress are not to be decided by reference to any formula which would give controlling force to nomenclature such as 'production' and 'indirect' and foreclose consideration of the actual effects of the activity in question upon interstate commerce."

The Court's recognition of the relevance of the economic effects in the application of the Commerce Clause . . . has made the mechanical application of legal formulas no longer feasible. Once an economic measure of the reach of the power granted to Congress in the Commerce Clause is accepted, questions of federal power cannot be decided simply by finding the activity in question to be "production" nor can consideration of its economic effects be foreclosed by calling them "indirect". . . .

Whether the subject of the regulation in question was "production," "consumption," or "marketing" is, therefore, not material for purposes of deciding the question of federal power before us. That an activity is of local character may help in a doubtful case to determine whether Congress intended to reach it. The same consideration might help in determining whether in the absence of congressional action it would be permissible for the state to exert its power on the subject matter, even though in so doing it to some degree affected interstate commerce. But even if appellee's activity be local and though it may not be regarded as commerce, it may still, whatever its nature, be reached by Congress if it exerts a substantial economic effect on interstate commerce, and this irrespective of whether such effect is what might at some earlier time have been defined as "direct" or "indirect."

Despite the Court's abandonment after 1937 of its role as censor of legislation directed at regulating the economy, as Justice Jackson himself acknowledged shortly before his death, the Court, "structurally and functionally, has survived [the] attempt by President Roosevelt to reorganize it so as to eliminate a 'judicial activism' which was impairing a program supported by large popular majorities." None "of the basic power conflicts," Jackson continued, "which precipitated the Roosevelt struggle against the judiciary has been eliminated or settled, and the old conflict between the branches of the Government remains, ready to break out again whenever the provocation becomes sufficient." Despite its retreat in 1937 the Court retained its power of judicial review intact, and, although abandoning the field of economic regulation to the elective branches of government, it turned its attention to other fields—political and civil liberties, the right of equality, and the problems of criminal procedure. The period of the Warren Court in the 1950s and 1960s would again see judicial power exercised as a major factor affecting public policy in the United States.

As Jackson had said, none of the basic issues surrounding the use of judicial power had been solved in the 1930s, and, indeed, such solutions are improbable as long as the United States remains a constitutional democracy with the judiciary possessing the power of judicial review. Such a system leaves most issues to be settled in the electoral process, but the power of judicial review gives to the courts the power to withdraw certain issues from the electoral process and to attempt to settle them as matters of constitutional policy. In the American constitutional system, therefore, periodic conflicts between persistent electoral majorities and the courts can be expected as inherent in the system itself. The conflict which surrounded the *Jones & Laughlin* case may thus be viewed as a more than usually severe example of the type of built-in conflict within the American system which had manifested itself before and which we may expect to occur again.

◈ Chronological Table of Cases ◈

Gibbons v. Ogden, 9 Wheat. 1 (1824)

Cooley v. Board of Wardens, 12 Howard 299 (1852)

Wabash Ry. v. Illinois, 118 U.S. 557 (1886)

United States v. E. C. Knight Co., 156 U.S. 1 (1895)

Swift & Co. v. United States, 196 U.S. 375 (1905)

Adair v. United States, 208 U.S. 161 (1908)

Muller v. Oregon, 208 U.S. 412 (1908)

Baltimore & Ohio Ry. Co. v. ICC, 221 U.S. 612 (1911)

Southern Ry. Co. v. United States, 222 U.S. 20 (1911)

Mondou v. New York, N.H. & H. Ry. Co., 223 U.S. 1 (1912)

Houston, East & West Texas Ry. Co. v. United States, 234 U.S. 342 (1914)

Coppage v. Kansas, 236 U.S. 1 (1915)

Wilson v. New, 243 U.S. 332 (1917)

Hammer v. Dagenhart, 247 U.S. 251 (1918)

United Mine Workers v. Coronado Coal Co., 259 U.S. 344 (1922)

Stafford v. Wallace, 258 U.S. 495 (1922)

Adkins v. Children's Hospital, 261 U.S. 525 (1923)

Chicago Board of Trade v. Olsen, 262 U.S. 1 (1923)

Coronado Coal Co. v. United Mine Workers, 268 U.S. 295 (1925)

Texas & New Orleans Ry. Co. v. Brotherhood, 281 U.S. 548 (1930)

Home Building & Loan Association v. Blaisdell, 290 U.S. 398 (1934)

Nebbia v. New York, 291 U.S. 502 (1934)

United States v. Weirton Steel Co., 10 F. Supp. 55 (D. Del., 1935)

Norman v. Baltimore & Ohio Ry. Co., 294 U.S. 240 (1935)

Perry v. United States, 294 U.S. 330 (1935)

Schechter Poultry Corp v. United States, 295 U.S. 495 (1935)

Railroad Retirement Board v. Alton Ry. Co., 295 U.S. 330 (1935)

United States v. Butler, 297 U.S. 1 (1936)

Carter v. Carter Coal Co., 298 U.S. 238 (1936)

Morehead v. New York, 298 U.S. 587 (1936)

West Coast Hotel v. Parrish, 300 U.S. 379 (1937)

Associated Press v. NLRB, 301 U.S. 103 (1937)

NLRB v. Jones & Laughlin Steel Corp., 301 U.S. 1 (1937)

Washington, Virginia and Maryland Coach Co. v. NLRB, 301 U.S. 142 (1937)

NLRB v. Fruehauf Trailer Co., 301 U.S. 49 (1937)

⋖§ Bibliographical Essay §⋗

Since the *Jones & Laughlin* case marked the beginning of the end of laissez faire constitutionalism, an understanding of it is essential to an understanding of the constitutional issues in the crisis of 1937 of which the *Jones & Laughlin* case was such an essential part. For further reading, see Arnold M. Paul, *Conservative Crisis and the Rule of Law* (Ithaca: Cornell University Press, 1960), an excellent study of the conversion of the legal profession to laissez faire constitutionalism during the post-Civil War period; Clyde D. Jacobs, *Law Writers and the Courts* (Berkeley: University of California Press, 1954), a study of the influence upon the courts of the authors of leading constitutional commentaries in regard to laissez faire constitutionalism, is also helpful; and Benjamin R. Twiss, *Lawyers and the Constitution* (Princeton: Princeton University Press, 1942) also sheds light on the contributions of leading attorneys before the courts to the establishment of a laissez faire interpretation of the Constitution.

For analyses of the general social and political thought of the post-Civil War period, consult Richard Hofstadter, *Social Darwinism in American Thought* (Philadelphia: University of Pennsylvania Press, 1945) and Robert G. McCloskey, *American Conservatism in the Age of Enterprise* (Cambridge: Harvard University Press, 1951). Finally, Carl Swisher's *Stephen J. Field* (Washington: The Brookings Institution, 1930) is an excellent study of one of the judicial architects of laissez faire constitutionalism and also provides a portrait of the Supreme Court during the crucial period from the Civil War to the turn of the century.

For an overall understanding of the New Deal and New Deal politics, see Arthur Schlesinger, Jr., *The Crisis of the Old Order* (Boston: Houghton Mifflin, 1959), *The Coming of the New Deal* (Boston: Houghton Mifflin, 1959), and *The Politics of Upheaval* (Boston: Houghton Mifflin, 1960). James M. Burns, *Roosevelt: The Lion and the Fox* (New York: Harcourt, Brace & World, 1956) is also useful in understanding Franklin Roosevelt's complex personality and the tactics he pursued during the New Deal period. On the National Industrial Recovery Act's effect on labor, a good source is Louis L. Lorwin and Arthur Wubnig, *Labor Relations Boards* (Washington: The Brookings Institution, 1935). Frances Perkins,

The Roosevelt I Knew (New York: Viking, 1946), affords insights into the New Deal's labor policies from the vantage point of Roosevelt's Secretary of Labor. The best analysis of the New Deal's labor policies, however, is Irving Bernstein, *The New Deal Collective Bargaining Policy* (Berkeley: University of California Press, 1950). Works that survey the impact of the NLRA are Harry A. Millis and Emily Clark Brown (eds.), *From the Wagner Act to Taft-Hartley* (Chicago: University of Chicago Press, 1950) and Louis G. Silverberg (ed.), *The Wagner Act After Ten Years* (Washington: Bureau of National Affairs, 1945).

The overall history of organized labor during the New Deal is related in Robert R. R. Brooks, *When Labor Organizes* (New Haven: Yale University Press, 1938). More recent good general labor histories that cover the period of the New Deal are Leon Litwack, *The American Labor Movement* (Englewood Cliffs, N.J.: Prentice-Hall, 1960) and Foster Rhea Dulles, *Labor in America* (New York: Crowell, 1960). The split between the AFL and the CIO is presented in Herbert Harris, *Labor's Civil War* (New York: Knopf, 1940) and more recently in Walter Galenson, *The CIO Challenge to the AFL* (Cambridge: Harvard University Press, 1960). Most of the sources on the impact of the New Deal's labor policies at Jones & Laughlin's Aliquippa plant as related herein are derived from the files of the National Labor Relations Board on the *Jones & Laughlin* and related cases. For a full citation of these sources, consult Richard C. Cortner, *The Wagner Act Cases* (Knoxville: University of Tennessee Press, 1964). Tom M. Girdler's autobiography, *Boot Straps* (New York: Scribner's, 1943), affords insights into labor relations at Aliquippa from the vantage point of the creator of the "benevolent dictatorship" there. A good study of the history of labor relations in the steel industry during the New Deal is Robert R. R. Brooks, *As Steel Goes . . . Unionism in a Basic Industry* (New Haven: Yale University Press, 1940), while Walter Galenson, "The Unionization of the American Steel Industry," *International Review of Social History,* Vol. I (1956), is an excellent analysis of the crucial organizing drive of the Steel Workers Organizing Committee and its ultimate success during the mid-1930s. The overall economics of the steel industry during the 1930s, including material on steel labor relations, is explored in Carroll R. Daugherty, Melvin G. DeChazeau, and Samuel S. Stratton, *The Economics of the Iron and Steel Industry* (New York: McGraw-Hill, 1937), 2 Vols.

The best sources on the legislative battle over the passage of the National Labor Relations Act are Bernstein, *The New Deal Collective Bargaining Policy, op. cit.,* and National Labor Relations Board, *Legislative History of the National Labor Relations Act* (Washington, D.C.: Government Printing office, 1949), 2 Vols. The history of the Liberty League, which supplied the principal impetus to the constitutional attack upon the NLRA and the National Labor Relations Board, is explored in George Wolfskill, *The Revolt of the Conservatives* (Boston: Houghton Mifflin, 1962). The history of the La Follette Committee's investigations of the denial of the civil liberties of labor, including the aid those investigations rendered the NLRB in meeting the constitutional attacks on its existence, is explored in Jerold S. Auerbach's excellent work, *Labor and Liberty: The LaFollette Committee and the New Deal* (Indianapolis: Bobbs-Merrill, 1966). The immense problems faced by the NLRB during its battle for survival are also summarized in the NLRB's *First Annual Report* (1936).

The best approach to the Supreme Court during the New Deal period is through biographies of the Justices who served during the period. The best such biography, and the one which sheds the most light upon the constitutional politics of the period, is Alpheus T. Mason, *Harlan Fiske Stone* (New York: Viking, 1956); Mason's biography of Louis Brandeis, *Brandeis: A Free Man's Life* (New York: Viking, 1946) is also useful. Merlo J. Pusey's biography of Chief Justice Hughes, *Charles Evans Hughes* (New York: Macmillan, 1954), 2 Vols., is also useful, although its analysis of the constitutional issues of the 1930s is inadequate and it tends to be uncritical of Hughes' performance during the period. Joel F. Paschal, *Mr. Justice Sutherland* (Princeton: Princeton University Press, 1951) is a good study of the most articulate spokesman for the conservative "Four Horsemen" on the Court during the New Deal. Robert H. Jackson, who served as Solicitor General and Attorney General during the New Deal and who later was appointed to the Court by FDR, stated the New Deal's case against the Court in his *The Struggle for Judicial Supremacy* (New York: Knopf, 1941). The court-packing fight has yet to be explored by any scholarly published work, with the result that Joseph Alsop and Turner Catledge, *The 168 Days* (Garden City: Doubleday, Doran, 1938) remains the most oft-cited source on the episode. Another journalist has, however, recently published an account of the court-packing fight superior to that of Alsop and Catledge; see Leonard Baker,

Back to Back: The Duel Between FDR and the Supreme Court (New York: Macmillan, 1967). Max Freedman, *Roosevelt & Frankfurter: Their Correspondence, 1928–1945* (Boston: Little, Brown, 1967) sheds new light not only upon the court-packing fight but also Felix Frankfurter's unpublicized role as an adviser to FDR during the period.

The briefs and record in the *Jones & Laughlin* case are on file in the Library of the U.S. Supreme Court. In addition, the oral arguments in the case as well as the other cases testing the validity of the NLRA are available as a congressional document; see *Oral Arguments in the Cases arising under the Railway Labor Act and the National Labor Relations Act before the Supreme Court of the United States,* February 8–11, 1937, Senate Document No. 52, 75th Cong., 1st sess. The Supreme Court's opinion in the *Jones & Laughlin case* is reported in *U.S. Supreme Court Reports* 301 U.S. 1. Works that place the *Jones & Laughlin* case in perspective in overall constitutional development are Alpheus T. Mason, *The Supreme Court from Taft to Warren* (Baton Rouge: Louisiana State University Press, 1958) and Carl Swisher, *American Constitutional Development,* 2nd. ed. (Boston: Houghton Mifflin, 1954).

INDEX

ABOUT THE AUTHOR

Richard C. Cortner is a Professor of Government at the University of Arizona. He has also taught at the University of Tennessee. He is a contributor to *The Annals* and the *Journal of Public Law* and the author of *The Wagner Act Cases* and the forthcoming *The Apportionment Cases* and *Modern Constitutional Law* (coauthored with C. M. Lytle, Jr.).

A NOTE ON THE TYPE

This book was set on the Linotype in Baskerville. The punches for this face were cut under the supervision of George W. Jones, the eminent English printer and the designer of Granjon and Estienne. Linotype Baskerville is a facsimile cutting from type cast from the original matrices of a face designed by John Baskerville, a writing master of Birmingham, for his own private press. The original face was the forerunner of the "modern" group of type faces, known today as Scotch, Bodoni, etc. After his death in 1775, Baskerville's punches and matrices were sold in France and were used to produce the sumptuous Kehl edition of Voltaire's works.

This book was composed, printed and bound by The Kingsport Press, Inc., Kingsport, Tennessee.